The Oxford Playhouse School of Drama always reminds me of my dire track record as talent spotter. I have advised two people to give up the stage . . . and both went on to be roaring successes.

The first to be warned off was Ian and Alastair Smith's kid sister Margaret. At Playhouse acting classes, there were plentiful chances to study Margaret, who was getting experience on stage We appeared together in the school comedy, *Housemaster*. To my mind Margaret had only two styles, either grand and rather camp, or sharp Cockney. No matter what the role, she seemed to make it one or the other. Poor little Margaret didn't impress me. I'd look at her and think, *'Uh-oh, you are not going to make it dear.'*

Very well, time passed, both of us had moved on to London, and I ran into Margaret, we started chatting and she unburdened herself. 'I'm not getting any work, what d'you think I should do, Ronnie? I don't know what to do, whether to carry on.'

As gently as possible, I said, 'If I were you, Margaret, I'd give it up.'

She gave me a funny look and said, 'Oh, would you?' For some reason she wasn't the least grateful for my wisdom. And she didn't take my advice, the fool.

Maggie Smith, idol of the theatre and rightfully so, Oscar winner for *The Prime of Miss Jean Brodie* and *California Suite*!

RONNIE BARKER

It's Hello- from him!

NEW ENGLISH LIBRARY
Hodder and Stoughton

Copyright © 1988 by Ronnie Barker

First published in Great Britain in
1988 by New English Library
hardbacks

First New English Library
paperback edition 1989

Printed and bound in Great Britain
for Hodder and Stoughton
Paperbacks, a division of Hodder
and Stoughton Limited, Mill Road,
Dunton Green, Sevenoaks, Kent
TN13 2YA (Editorial Office:
47 Bedford Square, London
WC1B 3DP) by Richard Clay
Limited, Bungay, Suffolk. Photoset
by Rowland Phototypesetting
Limited, Bury St Edmunds, Suffolk.

British Library C.I.P.

Barker, Ronnie, *1929–*
   It's hello from him.
   1. Comedy. Barker, Ronnie, 1929–
   I. Title
   791'.092'4

   ISBN 0-450-50813-7

TO JOY

the woman behind the man
behind the jokes; without
whom all this would have been
possible, but not half so enjoyable.

CONTENTS

PHOTOGRAPHIC CREDITS

1

ENTER AN EMPTY HORSE

ALL kinds of events took place during 1975. The Vietnam war ended, North Sea oil started appearing and Lord Lucan disappeared, Britain decided to join the Common Market. But enough of such trivia . . .

I was in Spain, and a big film. Not just a big film but a big, Dick Lester film. Starring Sean Connery, Richard Harris, Robert Shaw and Audrey Hepburn. It was called *Robin and Marian* and explored the Robin Hood legend, twenty years on. I played Friar Tuck.

According to the script they'd shown me in London, Friar Tuck was required to ride a horse. Now I don't like horses, not at all. Frankly they frighten me. This confession can be made without qualms, since horses never seem terribly thrilled about being ridden by me; the whole thing's fair and even handed.

"I cannot ride a horse," I had told the producer. Cue for soothing dismissiveness. I wouldn't need to ride, there would be a double for that. "But I can't even sit on a horse." Sure, fine, forget the horses. "Can I have it in the contract, then? Written down . . ."

This was received with a touch of pained irritation, as a lot of fuss about nothing. Why write it in, when the situation would not, could not arise? In that case, I countered blandly, there was no reason for *not* adding such a clause. Which is what happened.

After all, it was a producer, Sam Goldwyn, who remarked that a verbal agreement isn't worth the paper it's written on. And that eminent West End impresario Sir Donald Albery had long since taught me to be wary of spoken understandings. I reached one with him, or was convinced I had. Sir Donald was equally convinced that we hadn't, and I nearly went mad with frustration, trapped in a musical for two years after counting on being free within twelve months. More about that, in its place. Back to Spain and my first day's shooting on *Robin and Marian*.

"Great to see you, Ronnie," said Dick Lester. "I'm really glad you could do this movie. The scene here is that you'll come in on this horse . . ."

Aha.

"I don't ride horses."

"You're not *riding* it, just walking in on it, the horse comes on and you're on the horse," said Dick, humouring the troublemaker.

"I don't even sit on horses."

Directors know when to remove the velvet glove.

"That's crazy. You've got to sit on the horse."

Wrong. "It's in my contract," I explained.

Consternation, incredulity. "Rubbish, they'd never put that in a contract." (They'd tried not to.) "How can you play the part if you don't ride the horse?" he demanded. Even if I hadn't been a poker player, I could have detected bluff being called. Expecting as much, I had brought the contract with me to Spain. It was tucked into Tuck's habit ready to be presented.

Dick Lester wasn't best pleased.

Eventually, a few days later, I agreed to sit on the confounded horse. Grip with your knees and grit your teeth. Equestrianism aside, that film wasn't the happiest of times for me, though we had some fun here and there. But it kept me away from home for ten weeks, the longest period I have ever been parted from Joy, my wife – and I hated that.

A fair rule of thumb is that however spectacular any

film may be, the off-screen activities will rival it for suspense, intrigue and the rest. Never mind Friar Tuck, my main if unofficial role during *Robin and Marian* was as mediator. I became a buffer and smoother-down.

Think about it, Richard Harris, Robert Shaw, Nicol Williamson, Kenneth Haigh . . . those four alone were, shall we say, definite personalities. There were arguments and without magnifying the scene, something was always going on, little sparks of animosity. I can't remember between whom and if I could, I wouldn't tell, but in the end they tended to come to me. "He did this, d'you think I should do that?"

Interesting, yes, you could say that.

And in the middle of it all, oblivious, that lovely man Sean Connery. I knew him a bit better than some of the others because we had a mutual friend, the director Ian McNaughton. Years before I'd spent a couple of New Year's Eves at Sean and Ian's place in Camden Town.

At one of those parties Sean asked me about a striking girl on the other side of the room and paid her a bizarre compliment: "She's got a great stomach!"

"That," I informed him, "is the girl I hope to marry." Mind you, I dare say Joy does have a nice stomach.

"Oh," said Sean. "Ah. I'm sorry." And off he went. A true gent. My favourite thing about *Robin and Marian* was the lunch breaks under the trees where we all sat and drank red wine.

Perhaps it was the climate, the heat, but the wine never seemed to affect anyone. Sean would be sitting there, laughing and delivering a monologue about his preoccupation at the time – Britain's tax authorities. Two glasses, and he'd start on the Inland Revenue. "They're not getting my blessed money," he'd say. 'Blessed money' in a manner of speaking, his version was more vivid.

Denholm Elliott had money on his mind, too. Denholm has always been a fine actor and has achieved great success in the last four or five years, a lot of awards. He was playing Will Scarlett. The film people gave us our

15

on-location expenses in pesetas, and the daily allowance made quite a bundle. Denholm was saving his pesetas – maybe like so many actors he too had tax problems. But where to keep them safe about his person while in costume? He decided to tuck them into his codpiece.

Days passed, pesetas accumulated, until I had to take Denholm aside and tell him it couldn't go on like this. He was baffled, nonplussed, until I pointed out that his codpiece was, putting it delicately, giving fresh nuances to the financial term 'inflation'. "It's sticking out in front of your cloak these days," I said, "and I don't think we can have that in a family film."

Robin and Marian was made on location in northern Spain, away from major cities, so we were dotted around different hotels in the mountains. Denholm confided, highly pleased, that he'd moved out of his hotel and was living in, of all places, a monastery. "The food's terrible, but it's only a few pesetas a night."

Some days later he said, "Ronnie, I don't think I can stay at the monastery."

"Are the monks too stern and ascetic?" I asked.

"Not exactly," said Denholm, "but I'm absolutely covered in fleas!" He had to move out in the end. It's not quite the way one thinks of monks, being verminous . . .

One way and another, between the lunch breaks and the horse and the various undercurrents of feelings, the strange affair of the peseta codpiece and the flea-bitten monastery, there was plenty going on. But I was home-sick and the heat was brutal and I'd catch myself thinking, '*What am I doing this for? Madness!*'

And then there was Robert Shaw . . .

Gifted, versatile man – strong actor, film star, respected novelist. But he had problems and could be, well, challenging, ready for confrontations. Shaw had recently done *The Sting*, as the gangster whom Robert Redford and Paul Newman set out to swindle at risk of their lives. Anyone who's seen that film will understand that Robert Shaw could radiate power and menace. A frightening man then, a fearsome character. And he played on it at times, away from the set. Hugely competitive, liked to stare through somebody and announce, "*I'm going to beat you.*" It was part of his style.

So one day he joined Nicol Williamson and Denholm and me, caught my eye, and said abruptly, "You think you can play *boules.*" Shaw had been drinking, it was one of those questions which come out as statements.

"I have played it," I agreed cautiously.

Robert Shaw drew himself up and said, "I'll give you eight points and still beat you. For £100." It was, to coin a cliché, an offer one couldn't refuse, though I very much wanted to. The money was all right – it wasn't like the early days when I was delighted at Dirk Bogarde lending me a fiver, which supported me for the best part of a week – *but supposing I won?*

An eight-point start is about halfway to victory and Shaw had had a few . . . The game began and he reached thirteen without me scoring; then I crept up until we were thirteen each. Robert Shaw was fuming now, the prospect of losing put him out of temper, especially after handing me such a massive lead, beating himself as it were.

But he played a ball which ended right beside the jack or whatever they call it, the little target ball. (You can tell I'm an expert.) That was it, I had two shots left and if I couldn't shift his last ball . . .

My first try finished short.

By this stage Barker and prudence, a sane concern for self-preservation, had parted company. I wanted to beat him. Robert Shaw was standing there with that glint in his eye, and he *was* the heavy, the Sheriff of Nottingham, to my Tuck. In desperation, I fired a real bomb. Perhaps childhood years as a marbles addict were paying dividends. At any rate, it sent his ball flying out of contention and he'd lost.

A great cheer went up, because it was a very Hoodlike situation, the archery contest all over again. The Sheriff

17

was not happy. Neither was I, now that the spell of the game was broken.

Furious, Shaw slung the money at me and stalked off. Silly, but it was quite dramatic. I was a trifle nervous about our next meeting; he could be a bit physical. Luckily he was also a great fan of *Porridge*. Next day, there was no mention of *boules* and he was fine, all forgotten.

I love to see Robert Shaw angry – on film. I still revel in *Jaws*, and his acting in it.

Of course, *Robin and Marian* continued while all these sideshows went on. Horse or no horse, I didn't get on too well with Dick Lester. I'd worked for him on commercials and respected him as maker of the Beatles films and *The Knack*, yet couldn't cope with his way of directing. Purely a professional matter, by the way. Personally I found Dick Lester good company . . . at lunchtime. But I suppose that as a performer I'm what Americans call 'structured': need to know what I will be doing, what will be spoken, for what purpose.

Dick Lester didn't work that way. Generally he'd have several cameras going on the same scene, assembling and shaping his film when he got home afterwards. His version of *The Three Musketeers* produced enough material for the sequel as well, two films out of one.

"Do something funny," he'd demand on set. *Such as?* It's a crazy thing to say to me. He wanted me to invent on the spot and I was unable to oblige.

Our different approaches implied eventual collision and things came to a head after we'd finished work in Spain and returned to England. Dick called me to a dubbing session, where actors' voices are matched to their images on screen.

He ran a clip in which Denholm Elliott and I, Scarlett and Tuck, have killed a deer in the forest but hear somebody approaching and make a bolt for it. "What you say here is, 'What's that? Someone's coming. Better go,'" Dick told me.

18

"But my lips aren't moving," I objected.

"Doesn't matter."

"I'm sorry, it does to me."

Dick was dismissive. "People don't notice," he claimed. "I do it all the time in my films."

One of us seemed to be missing the point and it wasn't me. Half my performance was on the screen and the other half was spoken. Showing my immobile face with a voice coming out of it was pushing the public too far. Insultingly so, to my mind.

"That's crazy," was Dick's reaction. "I'm telling you to say those lines."

Ironically, my first work for him had been years before when I was doing a lot of voice-overs for commercials and films. When I explained that I simply couldn't bring myself to make talk emerge from motionless lips (Friar Tuck might be a resourceful cleric but ventriloquism was ridiculous) Dick Lester said curtly, "All right, *I'll* get it done."

We parted on less than cordial terms, after I'd dubbed other sequences where there was no similar problem. Despite the disagreement, I liked him. It was the director I was opposing, not the person. Joy and I attended the première; Dick was there, naturally, and we got along fine.

Funnily enough David Jason, destined to be cunning old Arkwright's much-maligned nephew, Granville, did a lot of dubbing for *Robin and Marian*, I understand. He may well have spoken for me in the "Someone's coming . . ." sequence. David's a good mimic. He does a wicked impression of me rehearsing Arkwright's stutter and then as myself – though he's never let me catch him at it!

So much for Friar Tuck and all that. What, for that matter, am I banging on about? Starting one's life story more than forty years after its beginning must seem a touch odd, but there is a purpose.

By 1975 a working-class boy from Cowley Road, Ox-

19

ford, had travelled far if not fast. From thrilling to films at Saturday morning cinema club (those Clay Men in the Buck Rogers serial made a permanent impression on his imagination and memory) to actually appearing in A Big Movie with even bigger stars. And he had helped to launch, in *The Two Ronnies*, a national institution of sorts, one of the best-liked programmes ever to emerge on television.

How on earth did it happen? We'll start finding out from the next chapter onwards. It is a shared experience because putting these recollections into sensible, what-came-next order (with an occasional diversion when the lure of an anecdote triumphs) revealed patterns to me.

How on earth did it happen? Luck, has always been my short answer. I was the unlikeliest candidate to become a jobbing actor; no blinding revelation, no deep sense of vocation from earliest years. Yet looking back, there were several little nudges in the direction I was to take, after a couple of false starts on leaving school.

First though, a warning to the reader concerning youthful squalor, agonies and degradation. There aren't any, though I very nearly died on one occasion. Sorry, but my childhood was distressingly normal and extremely happy.

In fact, if you want the dark side of show business, I'm not really your man. It has been tough at times, I experienced moments of despair and much genuine hardship. But my nature is such that, like the famous motto on ancient sundials, my mind tends to record only sunny hours.

And apologies again, this business of mine is full of lovely people. Nice ones, helpful ones, any amount of funny ones, quite a few eccentrics and oddballs. There must be some monsters and there are, without doubt, a number of pains in the neck. The trick is to avoid working with them, as soon as one has the chance to choose.

Enough warnings over what you will not be offered. Let the games commence . . .

2

THE PIERROT COSTUME

I WAS born at Bedford on 25 September 1929, Mr and Mrs Barker's second child and only son.

There had never been an actor in the family. Except my father used to put on his straw boater and sing for us children when we were little. He'd sing a music hall thing, 'I'm Not All There'. Recently I came across that song in Eric Morecambe's book, it was the number *he* used to do when he was a lad.

Father's names were Leonard William but everybody called him Tim. And Tim could be a Whimsical Willie. Whenever I picture him singing, he's wearing that straw hat . . . I wonder what became of it. He'd been an amateur entertainer at little local affairs but by the time we moved to Oxford, which was when I started taking notice, he'd pretty well given that up.

The straw hat, wish I had it now, was kept in my parents' wardrobe and so was his pierrot costume. There was a vogue for pierrot troupes after the First World War, they were part of the scenery at holiday resorts, on the beach or the end of the pier, and featured in village hall entertainments. Not just end of the pier, either; Stanley Holloway was in a famous troupe and there are photographs of him in the costume.

Father's big, baggy black outfit with the white fuzzy pompoms and the skullcap hung at the back of the wardrobe. From time to time as a boy I'd go and examine it. You could argue that a subconscious seed was being planted, ambitions kindled, but that would be fanciful. We simply loved dressing-up games and the pierrot suit was nice.

So there was no real family tradition of showbusiness: one grandfather was a whitesmith, a grander way of saying plumber, a gas plumber. He was my mother's father and Father's was a master butcher. My goodness, butchers looked the part in those days, substantial, red-faced men, no doubt from all the meat they kept tucking away. My maternal grandfather lived to be ninety-one so I remember him well. When I do elderly, cap-and-moustache characters I look very like the whitesmith.

Class was a factor when I grew up, it helped shape or decree many youngsters' futures. I'd say that we were upper working class. Father was a clerk with Shell Mex, as it was then. During the Second World War, on the borderline of being too old to serve, he learned to drive one of those enormous petrol tankers, a Scammel, and transported fuel from the docks. I suppose that made us working class for a while, in theory, since he wasn't a clerk any more.

I remember how we worried about him when he was in Southampton when it suffered its heaviest blitz of the war. I dare say he was worried too, driving five thousand gallons or so of petrol around in an air raid.

Father had an office job but he wasn't your stereotype little clerk. He had a great sense of humour. It doesn't travel well into print, he just had a fund of funny remarks, always there with a riposte. "Any fear of lunch?" he would ask my mother, making me laugh and her annoyed. I use it to this day, and it caught on. "Any fear of doing this shot?" I've heard a director enquiring.

"How many apples in a barrel of grapes?" Father would demand. Or, "How Hi is a Chinaman." That baffled me for years and years. It was only recently, belatedly, I realised that it was a statement and not a question. "Money doesn't buy happiness but it lets you be miserable in comfort," was another of his sayings.

People moved around a lot more in the 'thirties, earning their living. My father's job took us from Bedford to Ilford and finally to Oxford. My earliest memory dates back to Ilford when I'd have been no more than a couple of years old. I'm in a pushchair being propelled by big sister Vera, three years my senior. Obviously I'm involved in one of her games and Mother would have been keeping an eye on the pair of us. For some reason I am clutching a pot of jam which *must not be dropped*. It has remained a terrifying moment, and that pot of jam is life itself, as we career around the corner of the house.

We lived in a flat at York Road, Ilford, and the railway line lay at the bottom of its long garden. Father could hear the train in the distance, dash out and round to catch it by the time it reached the station. Readers with families will understand the fascination, the mild wonder I'm experiencing on realising that Tim could only have been twenty-six at the time. Family man with responsibilities, wife and two children to support, a train to catch – and he was younger then than my oldest son, Larry, is now. Yet he was Daddy.

Just as he was Tim, my mother was called Cis, something to do with being the younger sister in her family, a year younger than Dorothy, my Aunt Doll. At Ilford, Mother used to walk at least eight miles a day with me in the pushchair, taking Vera to school, bringing her home for lunch, back again at two o'clock, returning to collect her at four.

Another Ilford memory concerns the man in the flat downstairs, who'd tell me stories. We'd sit in front of his open fire watching the sparks whirl up the chimney. Soldiers, he called those little sparks, soldiers marching at night; possibly he was a Great War survivor. He was a nice fellow.

But childhood memories really begin with moving to Oxford and our little house at Cowley Road, near Crapper's – not Thomas Crapper the famous lavatory specialist, this was Crapper's Coaches. This would have been in the early 'thirties and gave me my vision of the era, the look I tried to evoke in *Clarence*, which turned out to be my farewell television series. Everything seemed bigger, wider, more spacious, less built-up. I suppose, because one was small – though it *was* less built-up. And there was much less traffic, fewer cars.

Most people, well, most people of whom I was aware as a boy, working-class people, spent holidays with relatives if they went away at all. I'd go to Bedford in school holidays, to see my aunt and the grandparents, in a terraced house in Garfield Street. Children played in the street and the arrival of a car was an occasion – "Ooh look, there's a car!" Recently I went back to Garfield Street and cars were parked both sides, nose to tail, it was a job getting through.

Bedford holidays introduced me to an older boy, a great lad, and his still older brother. They took me out after conkers and then they took me scrumping apples, a tremendous adventure. I mean we got through a fence and into somebody's garden and I was terrified, you could see lights in the windows. Well, I was all of seven years old.

More significant, in hindsight, was the fact that big sister Vera had a friend at Bedford, Barbara Whitmore, who lived opposite. And Vera and Barbara used to put on concerts in the garden. That was the first time, apart from childhood games, that I saw anyone pretending to be someone else.

We all sat on a bench, seats of some kind, and paid one pre-decimal farthing each for the privilege. Tell that to Keith Prowse! The girls sang and did high-kicking and all that. The little ones sat and watched the show; I wasn't interested or even paying that much attention, I thought. But a song they did, 'Keep Your Sunny Side Up', stayed within mental reach for the next forty years and was so much a part of that time, I made it theme tune for *Clarence*.

(I felt bound to alter part of the lyric, by the way. It doesn't scan and it pops up out of nowhere, nothing to do with the rest of the song. *"Keep your sunny side up/ Hide the side that gets blue/If you have eleven sons in a row/ Football teams make money you know."* The football team got dropped in favour of, *"Life's too short to worry, you know/Wear a smile and troubles will go."* Which was bland but less of an oddity.)

As I say, it made no apparent impression at the time, yet it must have done, if only, within a few years, to give me the precedent for putting on little shows with playmates at Oxford.

First, though, there was to be illness, hospital, and my first official appearance in costume – which scared poor little sister Eileen to death and thoroughly spoilt a certain Christmas afternoon for her. I suspect she's never forgiven me; or if she has, she never forgot!

We had moved to Oxford by then, where I was to do the rest of my growing up. School had started. The first day at infants' school plays in my head like a film: a hymn being sung and this small, shy boy sitting at a desk on his own. However, there was a little sweet shop on the way there – I can still taste the aniseed balls.

The next major memory is of the Radcliffe Hospital at Oxford, where I spent four months going on eternity, as an eight-year-old patient. I had nephritis, the kidney ailment, and nearly departed this life. Being so young, I had no idea of what was the matter or even that I was ill. I don't believe much pain was involved, if any, just listlessness. I'd drift off, sleep a lot. Possibly these were comas. At any rate, after one of them I came round to find three men standing at the bottom of the bed, our family GP and two colleagues he'd called in. And they decided I must go to hospital.

At first it was like a fantasy out of a comic. The nurse put a great big bowl of barley sugar sweets beside my bed in the ward and said, "You must eat a lot of that." Along came orange juice. "Drink all this." I was no fool,

I could tell that hospital was going to be wonderful.

Of course, within three days I was sick of the stuff.

And for a child a week is a long time, let alone four months. I was in for diet and observation. The diet was monotonous, to say the least: rice pudding every day, except for one afternoon when for unknown reasons we got jelly, and another when it was Christmas pudding, naturally enough on 25 December.

I was bored and a bit lonely, though the care couldn't have been better. Hospital became a way of life. Younger readers will be unaware of this, but in the 'thirties 'visiting hours' meant exactly that; there was none of this daily or twice-daily routine, your family came for an hour, once a week.

Christmas Day dawned and wore on, we had the famous Christmas pudding, and I became convinced that my family would not be coming. The nurses saw my distress and to cheer me up, said I would be the star of the ward Christmas party. They dressed me up in a Mickey Mouse costume – the suit, the mask with the ears – and I was delighted.

Then the door opened and in came my mother and father and Eileen, who'd have been around three or four then. So proud of myself and pleased to see them, I went rushing to greet my family, and poor Eileen, not recognising me, got the fright of her life and burst into tears!

Much rice pudding and many postcards to my mother later, I was taken home in a taxi. It was a shock, the house looked tiny compared to the hospital with its vast space, which had become my home. The house struck me as being about the size of a matchbox and they couldn't possibly find room for me in there.

Jumping ahead a bit, on returning to school after so long, instead of being put back a term I started in a class a year ahead, and simply stayed there. Ever afterwards I was the youngest in the form. When I took School Certificate, equivalent to today's O-levels, I was under fifteen. I remember thinking, with the precision one has at that age, "I am fourteen and three-quarters and I've got my School Certificate."

Mickey Mouse – I used to draw him, passing time in hospital. That must have been why they consoled me with that Disney costume on Christmas Day. And a year or two later I was still drawing Mickey, while sitting on a strange contraption, brown-painted metal, which had made its appearance in our new home at Cowley Road.

It was called a Morrison Shelter and was designed to protect a family if the house was hit by a bomb. I was sitting at the table, absorbed in my drawing, and Mother and Mrs Williams from next door had come in and were listening to the radio.

Mr Chamberlain was making his historic speech, breaking the news that Herr Hitler had failed to give certain assurances, and so forth, and that consequently we were at war with Germany. It sounded quite important.

3

DULLES DITCHWATER AND EVELYN TENT

I CAN remember the first time an audience laughed for me. It was at Donnington Junior School at Cornwallis Road in Cowley and I'd have been about nine years old.

A boy called . . . Thornton, yes, even his name surfaces again, was reciting the poem we'd been given to learn. Or rather he was failing to recite, stuck on a line and repeating it, praying for inspiration. The poem concerned a windmill and Thornton was going, "The swirling sails cut through the air – um, through the air, cut through the air –"

"He'll be bald," I predicted, "if it goes on like that, cutting through the 'air." It got a big laugh, the class broke up. *Aha*, I thought, *I'm popular*. Odd reaction, because I wasn't unpopular. There's a theory that comedians become comedians in search of popularity, to win acceptance. A lot of them have looked strange or had something wrong with them.

All that registered was that I'd hit on something funny and everyone except the teacher liked it. A terrific feeling. I felt really elated at igniting something out of nothing, making it happen. I got the cane, but it was worth it.

I would never send my children to a boarding school. It's wrong, tiny tots going off like that, especially to prep schools, just when they need their parents' love and care. It is inhumane and should be punished by a term of imprisonment. That is not a joke, I mean it.

That's not to say my school days were miserable. Nothing of the sort, I had a pretty good time. But I was a day-boy.

I'd won a scholarship to the City of Oxford High School, the grammar school, we couldn't have afforded the fees. There was a good mix of boys, fee-payers and those on scholarships. My chemistry textbook had 'T. E. Lawrence' on the flyleaf, in a childish hand – Lawrence of Arabia was an Old Boy. And Professor Heinz Wolff, TV's *Great Egg Race* man, was in the form above me. His family had fled from the Nazis and they'd recently arrived in England. His accent is much the same now as then, so perhaps he worked hard on maintaining it!

Academically I did quite well, generally placing in the upper third of the class, never the top. My little coup with the 'air-cutting joke at junior school was an isolated incident. At high school, possibly because of the war, we never did school plays, though the English teacher, George Masters, had us reading *The Merchant of Venice* – not acting as such, but reading it aloud – and I was Shylock.

That interested me, the excitement and elation were there. Showing off, really. Acting's just showing off in a sense, isn't it?

The masters were a curious breed; I expect they still are, for that matter. "Why is a mouse when it spins?" the Latin teacher would demand. The answer being, "Because the higher, the fewer." When we wanted to know why, he snapped, "Because it's the answer." End of Socratic dialogue.

"You ancient and decrepit old jackboot," was that Latin master's form of address to a pupil. We did have an extraordinarily eccentric lot, on reflection.

George Wright was a villain, he was awful. He'd be talking to you, and his speciality was slapping your face without warning. You knew the hand was poised but there was no escape. "Where are you going?" he would growl, if one backed away. And George Wright was uncannily fast. It was like the old gag about demonstrating the tennis champ's lightning serve – the person appears to be motionless, then they ask, "Want to see it again?"

Another teacher tended to bang boys' heads together and one of them must have been slightly mad, he kicked shins. At least one was more exotic than violent; if pressed, I think he might have admitted to a certain inclination, sexually. He used to wear a different tie on every day of the month and my friend Bill Fallows and I would draw them with coloured pencils in our French books. Fortunately he never noticed.

The prefects ran a bit of a reign of terror, but I suppose that was what they were for. They could keep you in, impose detentions. One used to torture boys, making them stand on one leg with arms outstretched for ten minutes, and if they put a foot down then it was standing on the other leg for *twenty* minutes. The masters seemed to turn a blind eye and some of us went in a deputation to the headmaster, who told us to clear off and not be so silly. "If you don't want punishments, don't misbehave." Faultless logic, no doubt.

Don't get the idea I was a sullen and disruptive rebel. All boys are rebellious to some extent. We weren't supposed to stay in the building during breaks but there were enormous window sills big as tabletops, with vast curtains: be sure that after the bell went, every curtain would shield a boy, hiding there for twenty minutes rather than conform.

We were forbidden to play football in the playground, but games were played behind the air raid shelters there, with lookouts to warn of patrolling prefects. I lived for the playground football but, that aside, sport wasn't my thing in those days. Now, I love watching cricket; but I then wasn't much good at it and preferred retiring behind the pavilion to play pontoon with a few trusty lads!

Gambling came into my life at a very early age. At

Bedford I discovered a machine which delivered two lots of chewing gum, every fourth time a halfpenny was put in. I would spend all afternoon waiting for the crucial moment when, after the third unsuccessful punter had got his single packet of gum, I could dash over and hit the jackpot . . .

I can't have been too bad a pupil because I played truant only once during the whole of my time at school, for reasons we'll come to shortly. I'm not one of those who say they couldn't stand school and, in any case, however much the masters clipped one's ear or used the cane, and the prefects harried us, one went home at the end of the day.

Home was, well . . . home. We were brought up fairly strictly but it wasn't at all repressive. Mother was always very loving and sweet. Father was the boss and, sense of humour or no, we did what he told us – more often than not. There were no dire punishments, it wasn't that kind of discipline. My father only ever hit me once and that was a spasm of temper. He was making or repairing something about the house and I kept on about something, hanging around and fidgeting as small boys will, and he grabbed this bit of wood and clouted me.

It must have been the exception to the rule, since I still remember it. As an event, not with resentment.

World War Two seems to have receded into the background, after Mr Chamberlain's dramatic broadcast in September 1939. As it did in many ways for Eileen and me and our friends. Food was short, that impinged on us. Along with Eileen I'd be sent right across town, four miles on a bus every Saturday morning, to buy six jam tarts. There was a large bakery selling broken pastries. It was an important mission. Parents were going short to ensure that children got enough.

There was only one raid on Oxford, as I recall; the story went that Hitler had ordered the city to be spared. But the sirens went, most nights, and we sat in our Morrison shelter. Once, the alarm was given with rattles.

"That's gas!" said Mum and, masks on, we waited. Then I glanced up and noticed Joey, our canary, tweeting away on his perch, perfectly happy and fit. Even at that age I knew about miners carrying canaries to test air, so I nudged her and pointed out, "Joey's all right."

My mother did a double-take, which must have been funny in a gas-mask, and then remembered that rattles signalled an all-clear or at any rate, nothing dire, while handbells would be rung for gas.

Inevitably, one grew sceptical about the air-raid sirens. "I'll be there in a minute," one would lie, when Mother called us to take shelter. I'd just said that one night, when a bomb *did* fall. I shot out of bed and passed my mother on the stairs, in my haste to enter the Morrison shelter. In a house small as ours that was miraculous.

The war ground on, but we children had our own adventures. I've always loved water, running water, rivulets, streams, rivers. I like watching the sea but inland waters, lakes and rivers, are my favourite. As a youngster I was always in – pun inevitable – hot water, for coming back from school with soaking wet shoes, having played in the brook near our home; it fascinated me. More than half a century on, I have retired to a converted water mill in Oxfordshire.

With a chum called Bill Strover, I made my own adventures. We'd go down to the river at Oxford and climb these enormous willows. It used to terrify me, that was half the fun. "This," Bill would state, very seriously, "is a pink funk tree." That was a fairly difficult one. "Now this is a *blue* funk tree." Meaning a real monster.

It was the beginning of lifelong appreciation for the countryside, despite or because of working indoors and under highly artificial conditions so much. I remember going out on my bike, at about fourteen, on a perfect summer day, hot and drowsy, sitting on a hillock in the sun, feeling the warmth, hearing the drone of insects, and suddenly awakening to all the possibilities, understanding how good it was, just being alive.

Onset of puberty is the unromantic explanation. It wasn't a physical onset, although unconscious sexual awareness might have been part of the sensation. *Life is marvellous*, I told myself, wonderingly, *and there's much more to it than I've known*. I hope that every boy has had this moment, sparked by the countryside; excitement, exhilaration, euphoria.

One spent a lot of free time in the open air, youngsters did then. Eileen generally wanted to be involved, kid sisters do. She had to do as she was told, that was the price of joining in! Mother would give us sandwiches and we'd go off on picnics: sandwiches eaten as soon as we got there, or sometimes by the time we'd reached the end of our road.

Poor Eileen had to assist during my snake-hunting forays. Grass snakes, I caught them and she had the privilege of taking the bag and keeping it fastened once they'd been popped in: "Hold this, Eileen!" I caught this enormous specimen, a female around three feet long, and took it to school. My desk seemed the best place to keep it – until the inkwell popped out during a lesson and the snake's head appeared in the hole. I have an idea it was during a French lesson with that master who had all the ties. He wasn't amused, there must have been a fair measure of disruption, and it ended in another caning.

At home, I kept white mice. Mother hated that. And there would always be a few tadpoles about the place. Eileen remembers ours as 'a wonderful childhood', so it must have been! No, it was, and we had a lot of good times, any amount of those happy hours for recording by the sundial.

Opposite us in Cowley Road were rather posher houses. They had garages. And there was a little service road for the cars with a turning circle at the end: that was The Alley, where our gang played.

Gangs seem to have faded out these days. Nothing to do with modern street gangs, juvenile delinquency and problem children. Just groups of kids from the same neighbourhood who made their fun together. Playing, in that sense, seems to have faded out too, for that matter. As youngsters, my generation spent hours playing cowboys and Indians, cops and robbers, spacemen and so forth. A fringe benefit was that children got out of doors rather more, I suspect. The problem was keeping them in!

Near our house was a tall metal column, probably something to do with sewer ventilation. The first boy or girl at liberty, home from school or allowed to leave the table, would bang on the pole as signal for the gang to gather. Like summoning the faithful to prayer: *"Let us play!"*

A slight departure from other games, was that we put on little plays. Already my great friend, Mike Ford, who was to become a BBC radio producer, was interested in anything to do with sound, so he looked after that side. I think he borrowed his Dad's gramophone and possibly a mike, and set up in the garden shed. He could peep out of its window and know when to put a record on.

We put a lot of effort into those little shows. It was playing but we took it seriously, self-disciplined enough to hold rehearsals at people's houses and learn our lines. The plays weren't made up as we went along, these were one-act plays or shortened, junior versions we'd picked up somehow and somewhere.

Eileen, being the youngest, got put upon. When we did *Cinderella*, I was Buttons – young or no, I knew the best part – while she had to be an Ugly Sister! That's another thing for which she's never forgiven me. Pamela Cooper was *Cinderella*, I must have been sweet on Pamela Cooper at the time.

In another of the plays someone played Dulles Ditchwater and Eileen got to be Evelyn Tent. She says that I was a leading spirit and, even then, paid a lot of attention to detail.

Parents came along on a weekend afternoon to see the

finished production, if finished is the word. One of the main things was the interval, with lemonade, and my father selling the strawberries he'd grown in our garden.

Putting on plays was just another game of course, longer running and more elaborate than most we played. I wanted it to be done right and go well, but there was no feeling of discovery, nor any sense of finding what I wanted to do when I grew up. Yet in hindsight, clues were being offered during childhood.

The first proper film I ever saw was *Bitter Sweet*, Hollywood's version of Noel Coward's operetta, starring Nelson Eddy and Jeanette MacDonald as the lovers with George Sanders, naturally, the suave romantic rival. Mother and Father took me to see it at the Regal, we walked past my beloved stream and it must have been an afternoon performance since it was still light when we came out.

Later, Ingrid Bergman became the first woman I fell in love with on the screen, in *For Whom The Bell Tolls*. Marlene Dietrich in *The Blue Angel* was another juvenile love affair.

As a boy I hardly needed films because I had wonderful adventures in my imagination. Maybe the seeds of acting were there in my appetite for fantasy. An Irish lady, up the road, must have had relatives or a friend in America because every few months she got all the American comics and passed them on to me. I loved them, the line-drawings and the colour, Tarzan always on the front page, Buck Rogers, Terry and the Pirates – about fliers, not buccaneers – and all the others, inside.

They'd be given to me in glorious batches of twenty-five or so. What pleasure and excitement: the smell and texture of the pages, the images and their style. I would get organised, sorting them into date sequence before following episodes through. I liked 'serious' stories, pictorial fiction, more than funny ones. My friend Ian Kempson had a big garden and we'd play out Flash Gordon plots there. The fantasies had such vivid power for me that still I remember a frosty day in Ian's garden, sun shining, when I could see all these weird science-fiction creatures, Clay Men and so forth, in the icicles.

That was partly the American comics, partly Saturday morning pictures. I can't recall much about the films. At eleven or twelve I went to the theatre more often. Father and Mother liked musicals and lighter things. They took me to the New Theatre, Oxford, where we queued for ninepenny seats, well under 5p in current money. But money was absolutely scarce for us in those days. The queue went up one side of the pavement and down the other and we could tell, from people's position in relation to a side entrance, whether they'd get in. If there were no more ninepenny seats when we reached the head of the line, home we went. Awful, after trailing all the way there, three miles or more on the bus, and not being able to sit up in the gods at the New.

I saw Alastair Sim there in *Cottage To Let*; no doubt his young protégé George Cole was among the cast. And a play with Celia Johnson, who inspired me to ask for my first autograph. It was a Guy Fawkes Night – fireworks were going off, there was that smell of bonfires as I waited outside the New's stage door. Years later I was able to tell her that she had launched my autograph collection, which pleased me and touched her! My path was to cross Alastair Sims's, fleetingly and in faintly rueful circumstances, as you'll discover.

The theatre was part of my growing up, then. And the cinema, my interest grew as I got a bit older. *Picturegoer* magazine could be hard to get, so I put in a regular order at the little shop near school. Acting, drama were a part of life but didn't strike me as a significant part.

There was no inkling that the future was to be dominated by the craft and career of acting – "Making faces for a living", as one actor titled his biography. That's what it is, really, at one level. Making faces and showing off. Looked at in that light, it's a strange way to have made a living.

36

4

THE MOST WONDERFUL FEELING OF FREEDOM

TOWARDS the end of World War Two, I played truant for the only time. My truancy opened with a long spell of suspense, right opposite the headmaster's study, which is not recommended.

It was a Wednesday when we had games, so it didn't seem quite as serious to desert. I was going to see Laurence Olivier's film of *Henry V* for the second time that week . . . and the cinema was just the other side of George Street, Oxford, from my school. Hiding behind a fat man in a raincoat, I prayed that the headmaster wouldn't take it into his head to scan the afternoon queue for the pictures!

Henry V had been made that year, 1944. (I believe that a real war being on, the historic war between England and France had to use extras provided by the Irish army, playing both sides.) Shakespeare's patriotic piece and Olivier's vision and talent made for stirring propaganda and the school had been taken to see it.

I thought it was marvellous, and Olivier became my idol, an enduring one. As an all-rounder, the complete actor, he is the greatest we have and possibly the greatest we ever *have* had. He can do everything, and has.

Thrilled and dazzled, I just had to see *Henry V* all over again and as soon as possible. Hence the truancy. The film was splendid but Olivier was the magnet. I'd been impressed, meagre word, by his love scene with the beautiful Renee Asherson as the French princess. There was a vein of sexuality there and in the nicest possible way it was arousing.

Dimly I could grasp how excellent that sequence was, charming, entrancing. *I want to see that again*, I thought, and broke the non-truancy habit of a school lifetime.

During my first 'resting' spell after becoming a professional actor, the New Theatre put on a pageant and I was chosen to play Henry V. Still a teenager, I was very nervous, but managed the ordeal by turning in a complete carbon copy of Olivier. I had 78rpm records of him as Henry by then. They gave me a wonderful costume and I must have captured somebody after delivering the "Once more into the breach" speech for everyone cheered – thanks to Laurence Olivier.

There you are, Olivier and acting at its finest had swum into my ken, as it were. But I was just a schoolboy and would have laughed or suspected a leg-pull if anyone had suggested that I might 'go on the stage'.

Peace, and with it, austerity, broke out in 1945, the war ended and my school days were about to follow suit. Having passed School Certificate a year early, the next step would be the two-year slog towards Higher School Cert, equivalent to A-levels.

Suddenly it hit me that I simply couldn't stand any more; here I was learning Spanish for something to do and I'd already learnt German, what on earth was it all for? I didn't yearn to take Higher School Cert, didn't even want to, I had to get out of there.

My solution to two years of intensive study was escape to . . . five years of the same. Maths and drawing were among my best subjects so it seemed logical, looking around for a career, to train as an architect. Alistair and Ian Smith, twin brothers and outstanding pupils at City High School were a bit older than me and a year ahead. They had already started at Oxford's architectural school, and I followed them in.

THE MOST WONDERFUL FEELING OF FREEDOM

The Smith twins had a kid sister, Margaret, just as I had Eileen. She'll pop up later, to my eternal embarrassment. Nothing unseemly, I hasten to make clear, just a scrap of Barker insight and wisdom I'll never live down.

Architectural school was a shock. Even after the discipline of grammar school with plenty of homework, the workload turned out to be fantastic. One worked from nine in the morning until six, followed by an hour's break, and then there were lectures until nine at night. Only five days a week, admittedly. More lectures on Saturday morning, followed by virtually non-stop work at home to complete assignments which had to be presented on Monday morning.

I couldn't take it. Moreover, it soon dawned on me that architecture wasn't about drawing at all. It was about the density of an architect, the weight of a brick . . . or was it the other way around? Strength of materials and so forth, at any rate.

After six months it came to me: *This isn't right, I'm not having it*. I was halfway through some lettering, I can see it now, and I stuck my pen in the drawing board and walked out. For ever. I got on my bike and pedalled away home, crunching dry leaves and scattering them. It was the most wonderful feeling of freedom I have ever experienced. Then I sat in front of the fire wondering what came next. That lasted a fortnight – not the fireside vigil, the wondering – until Vera, my older sister, made a suggestion.

Vera was leaving her job to become a nurse, which was what she'd wanted to do all along. "I don't think the bank has filled my post," she said, "so why not go along and see if they'll take you on?" This landed me the exalted position of junior clerk at the Westminster Bank, Cowley Road branch; in other words, office boy.

Possibly, though it's hard to imagine myself slogging through an adult lifetime of nine-to-fivery, I might have been swallowed up by the bank, to be spat out as Senior Cashier or Branch Manager after forty years. Pointless speculation, because soon after joining the Westminster Bank, another suggestion was made.

It came from a school chum, Geoff Broadis. Overtly a bit of fun, far more frivolous than sister Vera's practical advice, Geoff's few words were of immeasurably greater value. They helped to change my future.

"Come to the Theatre Players with me," Geoff Broadis urged. "It'll be something to do in the evenings." This would have been 1946, making me about sixteen.

The Theatre Players were a leading amateur drama group. (In one contest we lost, by a single point, to a company which included a certain undergraduate called Kenneth Tynan. Our nickname for him was 'Yellow Skull' from his dyed hair, unheard of for men in that era.)

"The Players are great fun," Geoff told me, "it's all jolly, we go and have a half-pint of bitter afterwards." Following up with the clincher: "*Lots of birds there.*"

At this point I must emerge from the closet to confess myself a practising heterosexual from a relatively early age. The reason that I can't remember too much about an early visit to Oxford Rep – which I was to join within a decade, setting me on the road to the West End – is that I was sitting in the back row of the Stalls with June Bowles. The memory is of actually holding a girl's hand, which was wonderful for a suitor aged seventeen or whatever.

Anyway, back to Geoff Broadis's suggestion. Lots of birds was exactly what I wanted to meet, after years at a boys-only school. There'd been a couple of rather scruffy, intensely serious girls at the school of architecture, no joy there. So far, courtship hadn't amounted to much more than waving to pretty girls from the bus.

It's pretentious to talk of enlarging one's social circle, since one doesn't have a social circle at that age. Teenagers had hardly been invented in 1946, remember. But that, curiosity apart, was a motive for taking up Geoff's invitation. I saw it as a heaven-sent chance to be introduced to the best alternative sex we have got.

Thank goodness he asked me, thank goodness I went! It was . . . terrific.

The Theatre Players met in a room above a furniture warehouse. The room was heated by an oil stove whose smell permeates my memories. And if I smell an oil heater somewhere else, I think of the Players. My first evening, I just sat there listening and taking it all in. I wasn't reading for a part, but it was lovely. Somebody offered me a cigarette, that was a minor landmark. "Well," I thought, "that's what grown-ups do," accepted it, lit up, choked over the thing. And I started talking to a nice girl, Pauline Kershaw, who became The Girlfriend for a while.

The Players staged something every three months, which struck me as quite intensive. Soon I'd be appearing in a new production every week, but the very idea of that would have shattered me, at this stage! However, the Players had their quarterly play, put on at St Mary and St John's church hall. I was given a role and my debut grew near.

It was *A Murder Has Been Arranged* by Emlyn Williams, a sort of play-within-a-play because it's supposed to be taking place at a theatrical performance. It opens with a girl rushing onstage and telling the orchestra leader, the musical director, to stop. He asks what's the matter and she announces that somebody has been killed.

Playing the musical director kept my back to the audience, which made it a little easier. All the same I was horribly nervous. In a great adrenalin rush, though we didn't know about adrenalin in those days, I apparently rattled out my lines with hardly a pause, only just letting the girl get her dialogue in.

Not a distinguished debut but we all start somewhere and I'd loved it, nerves and everything. That tension, the heightened awareness, taut nerves, spurt of adrenalin, never really left me, by the way. To the end, I was as nervous at first nights or recordings as that teenage self had been.

41

Our producer, artistic director really, Margarethe Bayliss, was mildly encouraging over that baptism. Learn to pause occasionally, if only for breath, and I might get on, she said. My next role meant facing the audience, the nerves and exultation were strong as ever.

Other parts followed, Margarethe Bayliss congratulated me on starting to "learn the value of a pause". We did *Arms and the Man*, *Blue Goose*, and then *Night Must Fall*. My part was fairly minor but that of Danny, the psychopath worming his way into an old woman's household – Emlyn Williams wrote it for himself to play – fascinated me. "Gosh, I wish I could play that," I'd think. No conceit, I wasn't big-headed, this was wistful aspiration, daydreams. I would play Danny, and at Oxford too, but not with an amateur company and not for years yet.

I played a spiv – rakishly tilted trilby, cravat, cigarette in the corner of my mouth – in *The Shop at Sly Corner*. My last play was *The Insect Play*, as The Tramp. A still from it shows me bearded yet uncannily smooth cheeked above the whiskers, striving to look older than my own father.

Then came my best role with the Players, in Pinero's *The Magistrate*. I played the son of the family, a Victorian scamp who smokes cigars and uses slang, despite his vain mother's efforts to pass him off as an innocent little schoolboy in short trousers. She wants to hide her age. I was looking forward to the part but never appeared in it, they had to find a substitute at short notice.

Something else had come up . . .

By now I had been with the Westminster Bank at Cowley Road for some eighteen months, making the less than surprising discovery that it was boring, very boring. But a living had to be earned, one went to work. The Theatre Players made it tolerable: the friendships, the preparations, the excitement, the acting. I helped paint scenery, helped with anything, worked unstintingly. I'd have lived on that church hall stage when we were getting set up for a play.

Yet it was still a hobby . . . wasn't it? There must have been some idea of taking it farther, since I applied to be taken on by the Old Vic drama school in London – failing miserably. No doubt my Theatre Players mentor, Margarethe Bayliss, coached me for the audition. I went up to London and faced the panel, giving them *Richard III*, the 'Now is the winter of our discontent' speech. (Olivier's famous film version wasn't out yet, so there was no help there!)

The panel included George Devine who within a decade was employing me at the Royal Court Theatre. Then George said flattering things about my promise, how I was going to be a good actor. I couldn't resist reminding him that he had not felt the same way at those Old Vic auditions when a seventeen-year-old in bank clerk's standard blue suit had tried his fortunes. "Ah well, we all make mistakes," was George's airy response. In fairness, I probably hadn't been up to much at the time.

The Old Vic duly informed me that I hadn't reached the required standard. My bosom friends Mike Ford and Ivor Humphris consoled me. Mike was the garden-shed sound expert for our childhood gang's playlets, Ivor wanted to become an actor, all three of us were mad about the theatre.

We clubbed together, bought a bottle of gin, retired to my room at home and drank the lot. We were paralytic, naturally, and my parents weren't best pleased. Ivor had his pushbike and my mother was most concerned over whether he was in a fit state to ride home.

"I'm fine, Mrs Barker, honestly," Ivor claimed, put his leg over the crossbar . . . and fell over the other side. That was the end of my formal training as an actor, over even before it began. I soldiered on at the bank and lived for the Theatre Players.

Along with Mike, Ivor and a few others I had some marvellous times. Thinking of them conjures up a magical, idyllic May Day morning. In Oxford, the choir goes to the top of the Magdalen Tower and sings madrigals

at six a.m. There was no traffic, at least in those days
there was hardly any, it was a beautiful morning and
the voices floated down.

Then we hired a punt, that's what you did that day,
and cooked breakfast on the river bank. Another friend,
Pat Dunlop, a funny, Puck-like character, cooked the
sausages and they were the best I've ever eaten.

However, I mustn't get side-tracked by nostalgia – a
powerful influence in my life, accounting for the tens of
thousands of postcards in my collection, along with
antiques and bygones of all kinds. Still, the next bit of
way-back-then lore *is* relevant. In that just postwar time
of 1948, fewer people, many fewer, owned cars. By the
same token, one person in every group always had one,
or access to it. They'd be The One With The Car.

When the Theatre Players, gearing up for *The Magistrate*, decided that it might be a good idea to watch real
actors and actresses on stage, our Miss Ray was The One
With The Car. She was the group's manager, a little bit
older than my circle, so we always addressed her as Miss
Ray.

We'd been to Oxford Rep, so this expedition was to
Aylesbury, where, illogically, the Manchester Repertory
Company was based. Quite a way from Oxford after a
day's work, but that was all right, we all piled into Miss
Ray's matchbox of a car.

An hour or so later the rest of my life was under way.

5

A CLOUD OF PERFUMED DUST

THE play we went to see was *At The Villa Rose*, based on an old A. E. W. Mason thriller about murder in the South of France. I can give no more information than that, everything beyond the title is a blur.

But the effect of it, ah, that's a different matter.

Miss Ray's matchbox did its stuff, we went in to the County Theatre at Aylesbury, not a theatre as I recall but a converted cinema, and took our seats. The first impression was an overpowering smell of the floral disinfectant which had been sprayed around. They did that in those days. And when the curtain went up, a great cloud of dust erupted.

No matter, I was rapt. This was a magic land and on the instant I knew what I wanted to be, wanted to do. It was a revelation.

I'd enjoyed amateur acting, it was a great lark, there was something about it. Now came this understanding that I might make it my career, get a living out of it, do nothing else. *"I must get into this!"* I kept thinking. Such a feeling of excitement and urgency.

The play ended, we fitted ourselves into the matchbox, Miss Ray set off for Oxford. We were all in high spirits, though for different reasons. They'd had a good evening out but I was absolutely euphoric over the discovery of my new career, a secret hugged to myself for the moment.

Next day I wrote off to Aylesbury asking for a job and enclosing a truly terrible photograph of myself, rising eighteen, in a black shirt and yellow tie. With horses' heads on it. Fortunately the photo has been lost but I thought it made me look great. I was the bee's knees in that get-up . . . and the horse's head!

I suppose that expecting to get a job as professional actor was unrealistic, cheeky. I had no background, no real experience, and was very young. It wasn't conceit; just the confidence of youth. An asset in being young is that you're blissfully unaware of the impossible.

I heard nothing for three weeks, feeling disappointed and in the end, a touch indignant. "Damn," I thought, "I'll write again." This letter said that if they didn't have a job, at least they could send the photograph back.

Almost by return came an invitation to see Mr Horace Wentworth at Aylesbury the following Monday, he might have a position to offer. Along I went – must have made some excuse to the bank or begged a half-day off, it being a Monday.

My interview took place in the theatre. Horace Wentworth, a cripple, was sitting there in trilby hat and the big overcoat. His first question was what experience I had, and he just grunted to himself when I admitted, "Amateur drama club."

Passing me a page from the script on which the company was working that day, he demanded, "Read that."

I began, and Mr Wentworth decreed, "Cockney accent . . . North-country . . . Devonshire . . . Scottish . . . Irish . . . Welsh." I did my best, and he remarked, "Your Welsh is very good."

I murmured something about not knowing why, I had never been there but liked the sound of that accent.

Where did those voices come from? How could a teenager who'd never been out of the South of England, supply them to order?

The answer is radio. During World War Two – I was

46

ten when it started – everyone listened in to Tommy Handley's *ITMA*, and I enjoyed all the plays, our family were great listeners. *Monday Night at Eight* with those mini-whodunits, *Inspector Hornleigh Investigates*. A recurring phrase from that, "Lit by a solitary desk lamp", is stamped into my mind. We still say that now, family private language for a fuse going or something.

Right through childhood I'd been soaking up the sounds of people from different parts of the country. I had an ear for accents, they've always fascinated me. Whenever we drive up the M1, I think what a marvellous project it would be, stopping every five miles or so, finding the archetypal local accent, and building up an accents map. Lovely thesis for some university researcher.

So despite being devoid of conventional training and having been turned down by drama school, in a sense I had been studying one side of the craft for years.

Back to Horace Wentworth, brooding, and a callow Ronnie Barker, junior clerk, awaiting the verdict.

"All right then, £2. 10 a week," Wentworth decided. That's £2.50 in decimal currency. More to the point, it was £2 below the minimum pay scale laid down by Equity, the actors' union. What a stroke of luck, not being an Equity member!

Quite casually he added, "You can start tonight, if you like." Already his mind was on other things, he had a company to run. It was fairly unusual, forty years ago, for a complete amateur to get such a start. Today it is out of the question, you can't get into show business without an Equity card and to qualify for a card – unless you're among a small number of drama school graduates each year – you must have experience. Catch 22, or which comes first, chicken or egg?

"Oh no, I can't start tonight, I must give in my notice at the bank," I explained.

"Give in your notice," he echoed, faintly sardonic, "so that's where you work, eh? A bank . . ."

47

"You're mad," said the bank manager, Mr Graham. He was a typical boss figure, very ex-military in bearing and behaviour. I'd resigned, either the afternoon of my interview at Aylesbury or the very next morning. "You're mad, are you sure you want to give notice?"

Getting my obvious answer, he played his trump. "Look here, stay five or six years and *you could be a cashier*." Impressive pause. "You could be earning as much as Mr Day!" Mr Day got £10 a week – we all knew what everyone earned, from making up the wages.

Mother was taken aback by my news. "Whatever d'you want to do that for?" Genuinely puzzled. She wasn't standing in my way or making a scene, it was simply that our sort of people didn't do this sort of thing. My father wasn't as discouraging and dismissive as Mr Graham, not quite. He did not suggest I was mad. What he said was: "I'm not going to stop you, and you must do whatever you like. But don't come to me for a penny, you'll support yourself."

Father wasn't being nasty, it was a challenge. Not to mention a warning shot across the bows, if this was just a teenage whim. Serious warning for a boy who'd never left home and was used to a close, supportive family. My father was saying that I'd better be in earnest; I would be on my own.

I think I met his challenge and won that bet. I never did ask for a penny, not even when – a year or so in the future, I was far from home, ill, and literally starving.

I joined the Manchester Repertory Company on 8 November 1948 and began rehearsing the role of Lieutenant Spicer in *Quality Street*, next morning.

There's a cliché expression, 'tatty rep'. Aylesbury may not have been the tattiest rep, I never sampled that many, but hindsight persuades me that it must have been there or thereabouts. I have never worked so hard nor felt so tired, so regularly. And I revelled in it.

One had to be young, mind you, and head over heels

in love with the life. After paying for my digs, lodgings with full board, I had 1s 6d, or exactly 7½p, left to cover everything else. And I was a smoker by then. Adbulla supplied theatre companies with a box of fifty of their cigarettes every week as advertising promotion. I was stage manager, in charge of such items – the cast didn't get Abdullas, they had Woodbines!

Oh yes, I was apprentice actor *and* assistant stage manager; helped to build sets, strike sets. And put up posters, in idle moments. The company couldn't hire props, so I trundled a barrow around Aylesbury borrowing what we needed. One curried favour with traders, which was pleasant if they were nice young lady shopkeepers, but less so when they were older and male, like Arkwright. Imagine Arkwright letting anything go without payment.

There were compensations. I was making a start, I was An Actor. Manchester Rep had seven girl students and that was fun – well, three of them were fun and four weren't and it was still more fun finding out which was which.

Not that there was much time nor energy for wooing girls. One just never stopped working. Time and again I'd ask myself, "When did I last sleep?" and unable to work it out, have to flake out before I dropped.

It was such a tatty rep that we rarely got full scripts. They came as typed sheets with your lines and just the final three words of the person before you, as cue. So you had no idea, if it was an unfamiliar piece, what the play was about or why you were saying something. Most bizarre; it became even more interesting when the typist lost her place in this skeleton version and dropped entire speeches.

Christmas was upon us, and we did *Red Riding Hood* for a week, followed by *Treasure Island*. For that I had to make props as well as borrow them, Aylesbury being a trifle short of cutlasses, doubloons and the like. That was in addition to playing three different roles, Billy

Bones in Act One, somebody else, a minor role, and Ben Gunn towards the end.

Well, as usual the work went on from dawn till dark and later still. While learning those parts we were putting on the pantomime twice daily – I was a comic policeman in that – and getting props together. The result was that I memorised most of Billy Bones but by the first night of *Treasure Island*, hadn't mastered Ben Gunn at all. No, that's a misleading statement. I went on, not knowing a line of it. Nightmare, the only time I've ever been in such a plight.

Understandably enough, I went to pieces. I knew that Ben Gunn was apt to ask people whether they had a bit of cheese about them, so that's what I kept asking Jim Hawkins. For some reason Jim was being played by a girl. My obsession with cheese, to the total exclusion of the actual script, rather put her off her stroke.

I'd love to have a time machine and travel back to 1948, see what those performances really were like. You judge by the standards and knowledge you have at the time, of course. It didn't register as tatty rep, to me it was wonderful and we were professionals. There was a man who painted the scenery, for instance, did nothing else all day – not like the Theatre Players, where we all had a go at it.

And I got my first fan letter, from a little girl asking for my photograph. That was a landmark.

But my goodness, it was a slog. At that age you can take it; even so, I'd be dropping with exhaustion, one never stopped. Sunday wasn't a day of rest, that's when we set the stage for the next week's production.

It all dropped away once I got on stage, though. It's an exaggeration to say that performers can dance with a broken leg, but not that large a one. Pains, headache, stiffness, discomfort disappear while you're on. If you *do* feel anything then you're not concentrating. (That's why it's so rare for anyone to sneeze while on stage; you have to be relaxed, off guard, to sneeze. I did once in

A CLOUD OF PERFUMED DUST

Irma La Douce, the West End musical, but I'd been there for nearly two years and was fed to the back teeth with it.)

My parents and Eileen came over to Aylesbury to see me. I remember my mother turning up and exclaiming, "You *do* look a mess, you must be living in that pullover." It was a grey, rollneck thing, invaluable for covering a multitude of sins.

"I haven't time to wash shirts," I told her, and it was the truth. I'd take laundry home with me in a parcel once a fortnight, travelling by bus.

The leading man provided his own costume and he had two sets of clothes. There was the check sports jacket and flannels, and an orange suit in a very rough, hairy type of material. It was *dreadful*.

"What are you doing this week?" he'd ask the producer. "Will it be the sports gear? Ah, good, because I want to wear The Suit next week when I'm the lead in *Rebecca . . .*"

One morning the leading man didn't turn up for rehearsal. He lived across the square, his digs were a room upstairs over the Old Beams Café, so they sent me to look for him. The proprietress said she hadn't seen him that morning and suggested I try his bedroom. Up I went, tapped at the door, no reply. Then came the sound of a snore, and I ventured in.

It was a deeply satisfying moment, confirming a theory of mine. He was fast asleep on top of the bed, wearing the wonderful orange suit. I'd always thought it looked slept in.

On reflection the Manchester Repertory was marvellous training, less in drama than survival. Don't ask me how I survived. I have a feeling my mother would slip me a pound occasionally, as mothers will. That didn't flout my father's ultimatum, because I never asked for it.

And I must have found my feet, since they didn't fire me. I even featured in a great success for Aylesbury,

51

playing the title role in *The Guinea Pig*. That was a West End hit, filmed the year we staged it, about a working-class schoolboy pitched into a public school as a social engineering experiment. Young Richard Attenborough had played it in the film.

Now the Manchester Repertory had another company at Rhyl, North Wales. It had the resounding title of the Armitage Owen Original Manchester Repertory. Why, is beyond me – Armitage Owen was a Mancunian but none of his players had ever been near Manchester. Perhaps he bought the title. Mr Owen wanted me at Rhyl to play *The Guinea Pig*, and I never went back to Aylesbury because it closed down while I was away. The rest of the company came up to Rhyl and we did *The Guinea Pig* there and at the Pier Pavilion, Llandudno.

Either Rhyl was a bit of a doddle or I was gaining confidence. My digs were about three minutes from the theatre, at 75, West Parade. In one of the plays I was a photographer's assistant and the costume was no more than raincoat and bowler hat. I was on for under five minutes. "There's no point in making up for this," I thought, "nobody will take any notice." So preparation was minimal and I knew exactly when my entrance was made, five past eight. I used to leave my digs at five to, stroll round to the theatre, don raincoat and bowler, do my three minutes, remove the gear and walk back to my digs. In and out in twenty minutes, the cushiest job I ever had!

That was the good news, it emerged. The bad news was that not long afterwards, the Armitage Owen Original Manchester Repertory Company closed down. It just finished. We all parted the best of friends and . . . I was out of work for six months.

6

CHARLIE AND THE BEDPANS

WHILE we were making an *Open All Hours* episode, not all that long before I retired, Frances Cox took me aside and confided, "I just wanted to say that you've no idea how much pleasure you bring to people."

Frances is a delightful person, a veteran actress and an astute lady. She made me think. I took her remark as a kindly compliment from a colleague, just what you'd expect from somebody like her, but when I acknowledged it in that spirit, Frances frowned slightly and, shaking my arm by way of emphasis, insisted, "No, you didn't listen. I'm telling you that *you simply have no idea* of the pleasure you bring to so many people, the good you do them. You literally don't know, and never will."

That's nice, and indeed when news of my retirement became public, my wife Joy and I were touched by all the letters from viewers saying how sorry they were, and thanking me for a lot of harmlessly enjoyable entertainment. Some of them said that a certain incident from *Porridge*, *Open All Hours*, a *Two Ronnies* sketch or whatever, had cheered them up when they badly needed it.

Some of those letters moved me to tears.

Everyone wants to be of value, and valued. And yes, although it may be blowing my own trumpet, I suppose that I have pleased a lot of people over the years. But I enjoyed it myself, that's why I did it! And if some good was done, then I was amply rewarded with the creature comforts of this world. But my cheering-up value as an entertainer was probably never put to better use than during my performances before a captive audience at the Wingfield Hospital, Oxford. I had come home to Oxford and Armitage Owen's repertory company was not only Original but defunct.

Just for interest I once worked out that in some forty years of show business I was unemployed for five weeks, after that half-year's 'resting' at the start of my career. There have been periods between series and times when I decided to stop working, but they don't count! (I've always been very lucky in loving work and loving *not* working. Working, I wanted to give 110 per cent effort and get it right, achieve the best possible result, but I am not a workaholic, home life and my family, interests outside the profession, have been equally important. Recently, when I began wondering whether it was time to call it a day, quit while I was ahead, that factor helped me decide.)

But back in 1949 I was trying to make my way or, strictly speaking, get a foot on the bottom rung. By the way, six months' unemployment wasn't unusual. Lots of people say that the *second* stage job is the crucial one. It's almost a pattern to get a start, then be becalmed for a while.

Not just at the start, for that matter. We were doing a *Two Ronnies* once, quite well on in the year, autumn, and an actor in his forties told me, "This is my first job this year." He was ready to give up, poor chap, and who could blame him?

Anyway, such thoughts didn't enter my head at the time. I bought *The Stage* every week and wrote off for every possible post and more than a few unlikely ones. It may have been during this period that I failed to make it as a Redcoat. Well, I was turned down as an entertainer at Butlin's, which is close enough. (Lighthearted vengeance was to be wreaked on Sir Billy Butlin, that empire's founder, more than twenty years in the future, as you'll see.)

Soon I wouldn't be a teenager any more, and mean-while I needed money. So I found work at Wingfield Hospital, Oxford, as a porter. Really one was an orderly, an untrained male nurse.

"The first thing we do every morning is screening," they told me when I rolled up. Assuming that involved radiography, X-rays, I prepared for something interest-ing and a bit technical. Not a bit of it. 'Screening' meant collecting bedpans and wiping patients' bottoms. A bit of a shock – it certainly wiped the smile off my face.

Screening apart, I was working on polio remedial therapy, in the hospital's swimming pool. Polio, infantile paralysis, was a real scourge at that time, though one hardly hears of it these days. It was a wasting disease, among other things, and sufferers could manage a little more in the buoyancy of water, trying to move their muscles. Heartbreaking, and during the initial week at the Wingfield I simply couldn't eat; it was that upsetting. There were two Australians who had been strapping young men, six-foot-four or so, and I could pick them up so easily, to ease them into the water.

I was still very young, of course, less mature. Though the sight of those pitiful victims, looking as if they'd emerged from a concentration camp, emaciated and near-helpless, would have demanded compassion at any age.

The odd part about working at the Wingfield was that from the start, when anyone asked my name, I'd answer, "Charlie". There was absolutely no reason for it, but I became Charlie. Maybe, subconsciously, I was making it clear that Ronnie Barker was an actor who'd be back on the stage any day, while Charlie was the hospital porter. I never explained to hospital workmates that I was an actor.

When I'd been working on the polio ward for a few days and the first shock had subsided, another young porter and I set out to divert the patients. I wish I could remember his name, he was a natural comedian, a very funny man.

Another strand of my luck, and I have been extremely lucky, is that I've encountered so many funny people. This chap still makes me chuckle when I picture him.

There was a door in the ward with glass panes in the upper half, only they were missing. Sister came round, we were supposed to be dusting, and my pal began cleaning non-existent glass. It was hilarious (the patients loved it) because he paid such attention to detail, breathing on thin air, polishing it, taking great care to work into all those awkward corners. And the pair of us had a banjo act with bedpans, empty clean ones, that is. Well, they looked the right shape, and we'd strum them, parading between the beds.

Full bedpans were used for playing football. The floors were very slick, polished daily, and we perfected this system of sliding passes. I'd say that it had the ward in stitches but that would need rephrasing. Bedpan soccer went down well, certainly, and we got rather good at it. This led to a moment, I swear it's true, worthy of *Carry On, Nurse*.

I shot a bedpan across the floor, the double doors opened and there stood not just Sister but the Matron as well. To my horror the bedpan went gliding down the floor, closer and closer, until it slithered to a halt six inches from her toes.

"Sorry, Matron," I mumbled, and made myself scarce. Whether it was because they needed staff, recognised the therapeutic value of a good laugh among people with no reasons for laughter, or simply made allowances for youthful silliness, there was no official sequel. I wasn't brought to book.

Teenagers tend to be idealistic, but I did have a sense of doing a service, being of use.

But I still wanted to be an actor, still pored over the ads in *The Stage*, kept writing away. Until . . . It was a new year, January 1950. Charlie the Wingfield porter asked for his cards, bedpans reverted to their proper use and young Ronnie Barker reappeared – as a mime artist.

7

BLUE CHEESE ON THE ROAD

WHAT had happened was that I'd spotted a *Stage* advertisement for "Enthusiastic people to start a mime company" and having enthusiasm to spare, it seemed made for me.

I went up to London, Haverstock Hill, for an interview with Clifford Williams who was launching this project. He went on to become a VIP at Stratford but then he was an ex-dancer with the Ballet Rambert. We met at Christmas time, and back came a letter: "Your offer of hard work and enthusiasm is accepted." At £6 a week – in theory, as it was to emerge – which was much what I'd been earning at Aylesbury towards the end.

There were six people in the Mime Theatre Company, including Clifford, and we rehearsed for about a month before setting off for Wales in dead of winter. It was a cosmopolitan team. There was an American girl who turned out to be lesbian, much to my annoyance, for she was rather sweet and attractive. And a German boy, a homosexual. So I was a bit on my own in the evenings!

Mime may be quite familiar today but not so in 1950 and it was completely new to me. As novice actor I'd been interested in the visual effect of posture and gesture; now we really explored and learned about it. My muscles were stiff in the mornings, at first, but after three weeks I could do a back-somersault, not from standing but a back-roll and up on one's feet. I used it only once afterwards, as a clown in an Oxford Playhouse production, but the general grounding was worth having.

With hindsight it's easy to perceive Clifford Williams's brave tour as adventurous, worthy and doomed. We set off with a couple of firm dates, two days here, a day there, and then everything was 'planned' no more than a fortnight ahead.

I see that one of our appearances was at the Reardon Smith Lecture Theatre, Cardiff, in Welsh legends, a burlesque of Victorian domestic drama, and folk dancing. Readers of a Cardiff newspaper were informed that we were "playing an important part in making mime entertainment popular in this country". According to another report, we were touring "schools and theatreless towns", places like Dolgellau. Sadly, some of the dates were virtually audienceless as well.

For the first and last time in my life, all of three weeks, I kept a little diary and it's still around somewhere. Weather is the recurring theme, cold weather. "Did show for secondary school, terribly cold . . . Terrible town, nothing to do, walked about all day, very cold . . . appreciative audience; *very cold*." The entries are laconic but tell a story. One mentions spending the whole night at a railway station, sleeping there. In the cold.

And we were carting this scenery around for the various playlets, just the half-dozen of us. On a Sunday we moved from North Wales to South Wales and had to make six changes, complete with scenery. At one point, having coaxed the stuff out of the guard's van and aboard our next train, we travelled in a cattle truck.

Horrendous, really, especially in freezing weather. The money kept going down, £6 to £3, then thirty bob – £1.50 to newer readers – and finally shares, splitting whatever we made.

Cardiff was the nadir for me. I got 'flu and couldn't perform, the others had to carry on without me. I was at 22 Clare Street, Cardiff, another address branded into my memory. Digs, of course, and my room was unheated. The landlady supplied me with water and I'd bought a loaf of bread. I was too weak to move. I might have had a packet of aspirins, nothing beyond that by way of medicine, and for seventy-two hours I lay there, sipping water and picking at that dry loaf. Bread and water: precursor of *Porridge*!

It wasn't a laughing matter at the time. I was in despair, deathly ill, at my blackest depths ever. I think I was damned lucky to survive . . . yet I didn't give in and write home with an SOS.

Somehow I recovered, and dragged myself back to Clifford Williams and the company. And somehow we struggled on, failing to "make mime popular in this country", but not for want of trying. We kicked around for four months, wandering as far as Penzance before going broke. Good move that, the farthest possible from home, Land's End as near as makes no odds, before collapsing. Six of us, just enough cash left for five one-way rail tickets – so we drew straws. Guess who lost.

At least the weather was much nicer, for it was April by then. I set out to hitch-hike home to Oxford, which wasn't done some forty years ago. Servicemen in uniform would appeal for lifts, few other people. Today, it's just as hard because drivers are scared of getting attacked; they weren't scared in 1950, it was just that hitching was outside their experience, by the time the majority of people noticed some pedestrian trying to thumb a ride, they'd be half a mile up the road.

It took three days and two nights to get home and a lot of those miles were on two feet rather than four wheels. I had 7s 6d, 37½p today, and 25p went on a luxurious night at a Cyclists' Touring Club. I couldn't afford breakfast, and slept rough, out of doors, the other night.

I'd love to retrace that route, but it was a long time back. I know that, wary of Dartmoor's desolation, I avoided striking across it and got a lift to Plymouth instead. A sunny morning found me walking and walking, and I was *starving*. (Ronnie Corbett has a fund of lovely I-was-so-hungry-that gags, including one about lassoing a pigeon which yanks him off his feet; there are special echoes for me!)

To my delight a country shop came into view, and that meant food. I had 5p left, a dozen old pennies, and something should be managed for that. Going in, I was hypnotised by a beautiful piece of blue cheese on the slab. Beside it was a basket of fresh bread rolls, gorgeously crusty, evidently hot from the home-baker's oven.

Mouth watering, I asked the lady the price of blue cheese. "Ninepence a quarter," she said, excellent news for that left three pennies, my bread and cheese banquet was assured. "I'll have a quarter, then," said I, watching greedily as she sliced the piece and took a maddeningly long time wrapping it in greaseproof paper.

Any self-respecting village shop smelled good enough to make you hungry, in that era, and needing no prompting, I was famished already. At last the package was arranged to her satisfaction and I added, "And three of those penny rolls, please."

"Sorry," she said with a smile, "I can't sell you those, they're all ordered."

Bread, then? No, she had no bread. That blessed woman didn't have a slice available! Retiring defeated, mocked by birdsong, I sat on a grassy bank outside and ate my quarter of a pound of blue cheese. Hers was the only shop there, one of those country shops set down by itself on a long, lonely road.

I got home to Oxford in time for my elder sister Vera's wedding and I wasn't destitute. I still had threepence in my pocket.

The Mime Theatre tour was, as they say, an experience. Some people might have been put off by it. After all, my first two theatrical jobs had died under me and this latest involved genuine hardship. Yet it never oc-curred to me to give up. Maybe I was too stupid to take a hint. From my point of view, I wanted to act, perform, I wasn't in it for the money. I wasn't taking a long view, I wasn't ambitious for anything in particular, bar more acting. So what was the problem? I'd get another job. Actually the hardship stood me in good stead, coming early in my career. After that, *anything* was wonderful and mere tattiness or inconvenience couldn't put me off.

Get another job. Easy to say, and in the event, it wasn't so hard. Within three weeks I was on my way to Bramhall, Cheshire, and the Tudor Theatre there. I was the newest member of Frank H. Fortescue's Famous Players, if you please. All the youthful resilience and arguably ill-founded faith in my future would be justi-fied, though I wasn't to know it. Bramhall was a marvel-lously rewarding, influential, formative experience, the place where I really began learning my trade.

8

A MELVYN CALLED GLENN

A WONDERFUL actor and very funny man, he was also a nice man – it doesn't always follow. He taught me virtually everything I know about comedy. Sadly, Glenn Melvyn had a stroke some years ago and is not in good health. We haven't seen each other for a long while. I owe him much, as will be explained. Glenn had his own series, *I'm Not Bothered*, in the early days of ITV and gave me my television debut, as well as the chance to write for the show.

We met at Bramhall, Cheshire, in the summer of 1950, at the start of my third professional engagement. Just turned twenty, I'd become one of the Famous Players boasted by Frank H. Fortescue. Nobody had ever heard of me! Fortescue and Harry Hanson were rival impresarios in the north, each had a dozen or more companies, so it was well organised with a central admin office and so forth; a good firm to get into, and I was terribly pleased.

Bramhall is a dormitory town for Manchester and the rep there was based at a converted cinema, the Tudor Theatre. I joined as junior actor and assistant stage manager, still holding down two jobs at once.

Somebody greeted me with, "You've got a lot to follow, you're replacing a very popular young man, name of Roy Dotrice . . ." And the leading lady was a certain Patricia Pilkington, young but forceful, very much the leading lady. Striking looking, attractive, but not the least malleable as far as the director was concerned. I never got to know her well, because in the West End or the provinces alike, there was a fairly rigid hierarchy with leading lady and leading man at the top. The leading lady had more status than the character lady; as character juvenile, Ronnie Barker was second fiddle and well down the pecking order.

Later our leading lady at Bramhall became slightly better known as Pat Phoenix, *Coronation Street*'s Elsie Tanner.

Glenn was leading man and would have been in his thirties then, but it didn't stop us becoming firm friends. He and I would go out after the show, the pub generally, though we never drank much. You couldn't get tight because next week's new play was always on the horizon and there'd be lines to learn that night. But we'd have a beer or two and drive home – Glenn was The One With The Car – parking just beyond my digs for a singing session.

We loved harmonising. I'd been in a church choir at Oxford as a lad, and Glenn was very musical – that's why I enjoyed musical items in *The Two Ronnies*. We would sit in the car singing away for an hour, playing around with harmonies.

The Famous Players were better organised but it was still *fairly* tatty rep. There were four men and five women in the company, as I recall. Glenn was the all-rounder, leading man, director from time to time, but he still had to lend a hand with shifting scenery.

Once we were doing *Dracula* and I was Renfield, the madman who eats flies. We were so short-staffed that as stage manager I had to put on the dramatic music for a particular scene – all done with gramophone records then, on the panotrope – pelt down a flight of stairs, cue the raising of the curtain and dash on stage to be discovered munching the odd bluebottle as it went up! Desperation time: four seconds at most to start the music, hiss '*Curtain up*' and compose yourself in a role.

All the same, there was a sense of starting to get on, at least exchanging one level of tattiness for another. And it was easy to learn from Glenn Melvyn because he was such a charming, funny, bubbly man. A fine straight actor, too; he played Maxim de Winter in *Rebecca* beautifully. *Not* in a fearful hairy orange suit, this wasn't Aylesbury any more.

We were friends, he was fun to work for and with, but Glenn wasn't easy on me. I was still going off on the bus, scouting for props and getting furniture. If they weren't suitable, I soon found out. "This is no good . . . we can't use that . . ." He'd give me a bit of stick now and then. Yet all the time, he was teaching me. It was hardly a conscious process, one wasn't sitting there with a notebook. I'm sure this happens in a lot of trades and professions – a youngster admires an older, experienced colleague, wanting to emulate him.

You could hardly help learning, it was a matter of picking up signals and getting messages. In such a small team, I was the only person likely to benefit from what was available – the women couldn't have gained that much from Glenn's techniques and approach, there was an ancient character man who must have known his business already. So it was all there for me, a priceless opportunity.

More fun than drama school, I expect. Hard work, though. For a start, there was the whole act of a play to learn most nights. The routine was to set the next production up on a Tuesday morning, decide where the scenery would be, and so on. Then you went away to learn lines, except that I would be chasing furniture and other props into the bargain.

Wednesday morning you rehearsed the first act, Thursday the second – learned overnight – Friday the third, and on Saturday there was a complete run-through. Meanwhile, the current play was being acted every night. Now you'll gather why we dared not get sloshed after work!

Hardly three years earlier the amateur drama group's schedule of a play every three months had seemed daunting. Now I took it for granted that we acted in one while rehearsing another – there were to be three hundred and fifty different productions even before I reached the West End.

It didn't seem outrageous at the time, it was the done thing, if one was in a repertory company. Though it was terrifying to see the posters going up around Bramhall on a Thursday for the following week's attraction when I knew only the first act and was still looking for the props.

The treadmill could make us stumble occasionally. I remember that we did *Harvey*, that lovely comedy about the man and his invisible rabbit, with Glenn, using an excellent American accent, as Elwood P. Dowd. (James Stewart did it for the film, of course.)

I was the taxi driver and for some reason made him a black man. I adored makeup and was always trying to look utterly different from role to role. In the end it became impossible, there'd been too many roles, but I did my best, so this cabby was a negro. Not very sensible, for it took me an hour to prepare for quite a small part.

We did three shows on the August Bank Holiday Monday. The Tudor being a converted cinema, scenery couldn't be flown – dropped in from above, then whisked up again – the sets had to be manhandled. In *Harvey* there was a main set and a smaller one within it for nine scenes. You'd be in front of the main set, then the inset, back to the main set, and so it went. Glenn was Elwood P. Dowd *and* one of three scene-shifters, along with me and another fellow.

By the twenty-sixth change, that Bank Holiday night, we were exhausted. We were waiting outside a door, heard the cue, opened it and walked . . . straight into the back of the other set. We'd worked ourselves silly, to the point of literally not knowing where we were. In a terrible fit of the giggles we inched our way around the scenery – there was a foot to spare – and managed to get onstage.

On or off stage, Glenn was witty, a superb ad-libber. It was wonderful working with him, though it could make me anxious. He'd ad-lib on the first night, and that used to wind me up a bit. Still, I trusted him to get the pair of us out of trouble.

In *Too Young To Marry*, another comedy, Glenn had the lead and I was his pal, a drunken Scotsman. By the end of the week-long run we'd added ten minutes through ad-libbing, keeping bits which worked the previous night, discarding something, trying something else. We developed a scene which used the harmonies evolved in the car, with the two of us performing a duet on the organ, one finger each. The audience loved it. He was such a delightfully, spontaneously funny man.

Random Harvest is a play in which the characters grow markedly older while the action covers several generations. So the players must appear to age from scene to scene. With my passion for makeup I loved that, 'greying up', increasing the amount of grey in my hair progressively, deepening worry lines and all the rest.

The snag one night was that while we got older and older, a butterfly kept fluttering around the stage. Not only was it distracting, but there were chuckles from the audience, tickled by the idea of a thirty-five-year-old butterfly displaying the secret of eternal youth and defying our careful illusion of decades passing.

The curtain came down for the interval and Glenn Melvyn set out in savage pursuit of that gaudy little intruder. "Don't kill it," I pleaded.

"Kill it?" Glenn panted. "I'm trying to grey it up!"

Yes, a lovely way of learning one's craft without ever opening a textbook. Enthusiasm was the key for me. Amateur is often a derogatory term. (Which reminds me of a chestnut: "What's your act?" "I chew hammers." "Oh really, professionally or hammer-chewer?" Sorry about that, couldn't resist it.) But I *was* an amateur, you see, in that word's bygone meaning: a devotee, an enthusiast. I soaked up everything to do with acting and the stage. Everyone loves finding out about what they enjoy.

Accents, dialects, turns of speech were as fascinating as ever for me, and that led to a strange episode. In the not so distant future I'd be playing Agatha Christie's detective, Hercule Poirot, but this was a genuine bit of crime and detection. As stage manager I spent a lot of time in the Tudor and was always in and out. One afternoon, making my way through the darkened stalls, I heard a noise backstage. Instinct made me wait behind a pillar, certain that somebody was there.

Sure enough a young man appeared and when I stepped out and challenged him, he said he was looking for – well, the name escapes me – Harry, say. "I'm looking for Harry, he's the stage manager here."

"No, I'm the stage manager," I told him. Puzzled, he asked, "Does Mr Fortescue have other companies, then? I know Harry's working for him."

There were other theatres in the group, so I took him round to the company manager, John, hoping for help in solving the little mystery. John gave our visitor the number for Edith Carter, the head office secretary, who'd know where Harry worked, and the young man took himself off, duly grateful for the trouble we'd gone to.

When we went in to the Tudor that evening, all the actresses' dressing rooms had been ransacked and the girls' jewellery was missing. The man had been a crook. And he'd conned his way free, chatting to me with his pockets full of stolen property, hadn't panicked, came round to the manager with me, wrote down Edith Carter's phone number.

The police wanted his description, but he'd been average, nondescript, as far as I remembered. I hadn't thought much of it at the time we were concentrating on helping him find his friend.

"One thing though," I said, "he had a strange accent, an unusual one and I know it."

What accent? Ah, I couldn't think, but assured them it would come to me and I'd be in touch. Back at my digs I realised that it had been a Rhyl or Llandudno accent, I recognised it from having worked there.

Some weeks afterwards the police contacted me to say they'd caught the fellow. He was the son of an actress who'd toured with her and knew his way around theatres. He'd learned that in those days when there was less security (not to mention less crime) people did wander in and out during the day. They'd have a hard time now!

"We knew he was the one as soon as he admitted where he came from," the CID man explained. "Colwyn Bay." Which is right between Rhyl and Llandudno, on the same ten miles or so of coastline. My ear for accents had been reliable; the thief can't have admired it.

That spell at Bramhall was immensely formative, theatrically and generally. I learned to love north-country people, marvellous folk. Making *Open All Hours* was all the more enjoyable for the location work up there.

Professionally, I had gained a little experience, a measure of poise. My face started fitting, people got to know me; that felt nice. A local paper review said I was taking character parts in my stride.

Oh yes, and Bramhall was where I learned to play billiards and snooker. *Too Young To Marry*, in which Glenn, the audience and I had enjoyed ourselves, was my final play there. On Saturday night, the last, an admirer presented me with a billiard cue. But that same local paper refers to the recipient as "popular young *Robin* Barker", so there was no danger of mistaking myself for a household name, even in Bramhall households!

I'd been doing well, was beginning to make an impression, loved the work and had no driving ambition beyond getting a reasonable part in the next week's play. So why in the world was I quitting?

Fairly frivolous reasons, to be honest. It turned out to be one of those crossroads, a crucial career move, but except for earning a living, I wasn't thinking of career moves. Before we go into all that, there will be a short intermission. Or a digression, anyway.

9

MR WILEY, I PRESUME?

LET's desert chronological order for a little while, jumping ahead a few years and then lots of years. This chapter
partly involves Glenn Melvyn and brings another strand
into the story, scriptwriting. I still consider myself a
better doctor of other people's scripts – it's easier, for
one thing! – more tinkerer than composer. However, I
have turned out about two hundred sketches and written
a number of episodes for series.

Indirectly the seeds were planted at Bramhall, simply
through knowing Glenn Melvyn. Soon after the birth of
ITV, he got his own series and more were to follow, *I'm
Not Bothered* giving way to *Beside The Seaside* and *Under
New Management*. And he'd written stage plays, including *The Love Match*. That was a hit for Arthur Askey,
running two years in London.

By the mid-1950s Glenn was a national name, successful and affluent.

My arrival in London as a struggling actor and small
fish in a big pond, was Bramhall all over again. And
again, dear Glenn Melvyn was a good supportive friend.
He and his wife took me out, there were meals at expensive restaurants, and he gave me my television debut on
I'm Not Bothered, in 1956. Rediffusion, the old London-
based weekday channel, made that show. (In 1968 *my*
first series, *The Ronnie Barker Playhouse*, went out from
Rediffusion and it was nice to have Glenn acting with

70

me in an urban-cowboys episode called 'The Fastest Gun In Finchley'.)

It was a big thing for me, going on television for the first time. Sleep was difficult the night before. I was terrified over 'the moves'. This was a new medium and 'the legitimate theatre' was full of rumours and horror stories about the moves being paramount: miss your mark on the studio floor and a show could be ruined, you would never work on television again.

It was rubbish, as a matter of fact. All the same, I was hugely relieved to find myself playing a bedbound hospital patient with no moves! That led on to ghost-writing for Glenn, another first. Obviously it was done anonymously.

Henry Kendall, who had been a noted light comedy actor, directed some of those *I'm Not Bothered* episodes. He was getting older then. Henry didn't know I was working on the scripts and he was pretty dismissive of me. He saw me as a hanger-on, taking advantage of having known Glenn Melvyn in his northern repertory theatre days.

After one of the shows ended I ventured, "That went well, Mr Kendall."

And he nodded in a patronising way and agreed, "Well, there was a bit of quality in the writing, laddie." Wagging a finger. "Yes, a bit of quality in the writing." It made me very proud, there was a definite glow, especially since he was unaware of complimenting me, so it had to be sincere.

Fast-forwarding to 1965, by which time I had a lot of radio experience and quite a bit on television, I returned to repertory of a kind, but on the box. *Gaslight Theatre* was a BBC Light Entertainment project, and a lovely idea – Victorian melodramas presented in a theatre before a live audience, with a regular company including Alfred Marks, Warren Mitchell, Eira Heath and myself. Kate O'Mara was in at least one of them, maybe more. All the old favourites, *Maria Marten, Sweeny Todd, The Worst*

Woman in London, with the audience urged to hiss the villain, cheer the hero.

They had an hour-long slot, and that was the rub. Alec Clunes, a distinguished actor with great knowledge and affection for the material, was adapting the scripts and producing the series. At the first read-through, it took us two hours and Alec said, "Not to worry, I'll bring cuts in tomorrow."

Which he did.

Alec dictated the cuts, Warren and I exchanged glances. We were removing four words and replacing them with one, here and there. The subsequent read-through lasted one hour and fifty minutes. It went on like that for days as Alec, bless him, pruned gingerly. Rehearsals lasted a fortnight and the outcome was that, only three days before doing the programme, we weren't sure of the final script.

Putting it mildly, this failed to boost confidence and didn't make our job any easier. It was just the same before the second episode; the read-through for the third finished after two hours – and something snapped.

"Right-oh, Alex, give us a ring when it's down to an hour, and I'll be back." It wasn't my style, I had never done anything like that before. There was a stunned silence and I went home. Warren Mitchell phoned saying it had needed doing, "But will it do the trick?"

Then Alec Clunes rang. Naturally I apologised, he was such a nice man and I felt bad, but as I explained, we couldn't go on this way. There was a short silence and he asked, "D'you think *you* could cut it to an hour?"

"I'll have a go." I sat down with the script and realised that it had two stories all the way through, fifty per cent more than there was time for, so one had to go. Alec was nonplussed when I pointed this out, because Bill Owen and Megs Jenkins had been booked for the scrapped segment. (They got paid, anyway; I argued that they must be, since they would have been, had there been dialogue for them to deliver.)

After that, I worked on the final three plays of the season and really enjoyed it. Cutting rather than writing. If I hadn't been an actor I would have loved film editing. When possible sketches, bits of dialogue, occurred to me while working in David Frost's TV programmes, I still felt wary about submitting them. I was inexperienced, after all, and David used the best writers around. Hence Gerald Wiley . . .

Wiley's story has been told many times, and embroidered. It wasn't a practical joke and I wasn't being clever – quite the reverse. Having written a sketch, I wanted it to be judged on its own merit. Had I given it to the programme openly, it could have been embarrassing for both parties. They'd find it hard to reject something from a member of the team and I winced at imagining the stalling – "Yes, very good, we'll have to see whether that can be fitted in . . ."

What's more, there is a lot of hyperbole and stroking, as they call it, in showbusiness. It can be hard to get straight talk and be sure of what people really think of you and your work. Believe everything that's said, especially on the flattering side, and you'd be very foolish. I've always been grateful for compliments but results are what count. If they ask you to do another series, *then* you know the last one must have been all right or better.

So I submitted that first sketch under the pseudonym of Gerald Wiley. It was an ugly sort of name, I wanted something that looked genuine, and reasoned that nobody would *pick* Gerald Wiley, it would have had to have been given them before they had any say over it.

Friends and colleagues didn't know, not even Ronnie Corbett. I really worked under deep cover. My agent, Peter Eade, helped by sending the script in "on behalf of a client", and telling the production people that Wiley was a novelist, shy and reclusive. Peter managed to imply that our Gerald might be gay: "He's a bit, er, precious, you know . . . relaxes by writing this sort of thing."

And it worked a treat, nobody tumbled, the sketch was accepted. I kept writing more. It worked so well that by the third week they rejected my offering, or Gerald Wiley's, saying it wasn't up to scratch. That was satisfying in a perverse way, for it proved my original point.

Ronnie C. loved one sketch and wanted to buy it for his cabaret act. He asked me for advice, wondering whether Wiley would sell the material, confiding the price he would offer. "Too much," I said, "it's worth only half that. Depend on it, this chap will snap up less, be glad of the money!"

People became intrigued by Gerald Wiley, started wondering about him. Towards the end of that season, I let it be known that Wiley wanted to meet us all, and would host an end-of-show dinner at a restaurant near the studios. All sorts of theories were flying around on the night, some bets were on Tom Stoppard, some on Pinter. We all sat there, staring at the vacant chair. When finally I stood up and disclosed Wiley's true identity it was something of an anticlimax. Not everyone believed me at first.

After that, Wiley was blown so I chose a string of different names over the years: Jonathan Cobbold, Goetz, and for *Clarence* – the final series, about the bat-blind removal man in a 'thirties country setting – I became Bob Ferris. Having been accepted as a writer I could have dropped the pen-names but the idea never appealed to me. I didn't want to be accused of that Charlie Chaplin, Orson Welles thing, the 'written by and starring' trip.

Gerald Wiley lived on, incidentally, getting his own Television Centre dressing room when *The Two Ronnies* was in production there. Set between Ronnie C.'s and mine, we used it for after-show entertainment of family and friends.

I didn't crave recognition as a writer, I was happy to sit on the sidelines. Sit very still, pretending you are not there, and people tend not to see you. That was the idea of unflamboyant pseudonyms. If the script went down well, satisfaction did not depend on jumping up and shouting, "That was me, that was me."

From a self-serving viewpoint, hogging every possible credit lays one open to maximum stick, as well! My mother didn't take to *Clarence*, for instance. What a disaster, when one's own mother is unimpressed. "I don't think it's very funny," she said, "but I suppose you have to say what the writer puts into your mouth, dear."

"Quite right," I agreed meekly. The fact that it turned out to be one of my most popular characterisations means little to her, bless her heart. She had every right not to think it funny. Thank goodness that seventeen million other viewers thought differently!

10

CAN'T HEAR YOU, LOVELY HEARTS!

BACK to Bramhall and a certain young character actor.

On the eve of going to Aylesbury, turning professional, I'd been on a bus with my chum Ivor Humphris going down Broad Street, Oxford. Ivor wanted to be an actor, too; this great make-or-break adventure on which I was embarking must have dominated our thoughts. He turned to me and said, "Look, Ronnie, if you ever make it to the West End, *don't get blasé.*" Well, one said things like that at our age.

It made me laugh, then. The West End was beyond my ken, getting there was unimaginable. Blasé? It would be too marvellous for that.

With Aylesbury, the mime theatre tour and now the best part of two years at the Tudor Theatre under my belt, getting to London was no longer unimaginable but it seemed just as far away. I wanted to get there, wanted to be a success, but the future was still next week . . . would I be able to find those vital props in time?

Some entertainers make no bones over having had driving ambition, and being ready to stand on others' hands if needs be to mount the ladder. My goals were more limited: to get better at what I was doing, and work steadily in things I liked. Obviously there are many different roads to the same destination.

I liked Aylesbury, but then Ivor Humphris wrote to me. "I've got into the repertory company at Oxford as a publicity man and I'm also playing, would you believe it, Barker in *When Knights Were Bold*, our Christmas show."

Ivor's letter was full of news from home. Mike Ford, our mutual friend and sound expert for The Alley Gang's back-garden productions, had got in as well, working the Oxford Playhouse's panotrope, the sound system of those days. And Ivor mentioned that it was only one play per fortnight at the Playhouse instead of the weekly routine at Bramhall.

I wonder what they do in the second week? I asked myself, thinking of the luxury of all that extra time between productions. And Oxford was my home town. And Ivor and Mike were in the company, two musketeers needing a third. But that was just a daydream, not much more than a passing thought on 'wouldn't-it-be-lovely' lines.

Luckily Mike Ford was a bit more forceful than Ivor or me. "Write to Frank Shelley," he suggested, "and I'll have a word with him, say that you're worth seeing." That was brave of Mike, because Frank Shelley ran the Oxford Playhouse and nobody was in any doubt of the fact. He was the director, and appeared on stage; a godlike figure and he could be a terrifying man, especially to youngsters.

So I did write and Mike was good as his word. Minion and young whippersnapper or no, he did approach Frank Shelley on my behalf. "And he'll see you next Monday, Ronnie."

I got a week off from Bramhall, hurried home to Oxford and – Frank Shelley said he couldn't give me a job. That was the bad news. The good wasn't all that good, but . . .

"I've got no acting jobs but I could do with another person on publicity, I'm very keen on publicity," he boomed. "Now have you ever done publicity?"

77

I'd have been a fool to say no, and having handed out leaflets at Aylesbury ("Come to *Rebecca* and the egregious hairy orange suit"), saying yes was a white lie. Frank immediately called my bluff. "Tell you what I'll do, get a notebook, look around the theatre here, find me three very good publicity ideas and tell them to me at eleven a.m. tomorrow."

Actually I worked out a dozen ideas, from better use of advertising space on the front of the Playhouse, to special books of matches, that sort of thing. Frank Shelley liked about five of them, but once more there was good news and bad news.

"Excellent, all right, you can work here. What are they paying you at Bramhall?" Cue for my second fib, a £2 one this time, claiming that I'd been getting £8 instead of £6 a week.

"Can't pay that, out of the question, I'll give you £3 a week."

That was a bit rich – or rather, it was nothing of the kind – it took me aback and even Frank was a touch defensive. "Um, I know it's very little but that's all I can afford at the moment."

Those last three words were grounds for hope, I proposed that if I turned out to be any good he should pay me £5, Frank remarked, "Why not?" and I had a new job. Fiercely ambitious people aren't notorious for taking pay-cuts when changing employers; I moved for the sake of home comforts – Mother doing my laundry, all the domestic side taken care of – and being with my schooldays friends. It made no sense 'career-wise' . . . and was one of the best moves I could have made. Even though I appeared to have taken one halting step forward and two back, dropping from actor to assistant publicist.

The tasks were pretty menial, handing out leaflets, working my way up to dizzy heights of designing posters, arranging window displays in local shops. But after three weeks Frank Shelley came in and rumbled –

he had this very deep, imposing, sense-of-occasion voice, he *spoke* like an actor-manager.

"I'm doing a play with a very large cast, very large, and there's a small part . . . I wonder . . . You could probably do it, if you're interested."

"Yes please!"

Pick-up Girl, an American courtroom drama, was a very good play with a very bad title. The central character's accused of immorality but she is a victim of rumour and prejudice, misjudgement. My role was Peter Marti, a young musician, witness for the defence. He loves her, knows the girl's true worth and speaks up for her.

As Frank said, it was a small part but quite important to the play's development. Marti has two good scenes, one of them springing a surprise in the plot, so a lot could be made of it. It isn't vanity to claim that in all the time I was at Oxford, I never gave a better performance. I was so keen to make an impression – on Frank Shelley as much as the audience, though it came to the same thing – so that he would realise that I was an actor.

It worked, thank goodness. Donald Hewlett, the leading man – the CO in *It Ain't Half Hot, Mum* on BBC 1, sundry years later – said I was marvellous, the whole cast was very kind, the local critics noticed me. Just passing references to an interesting new young player, but it was enough. One way and another, Frank Shelley got the message and I never went back to the publicity department.

Frank Shelley was a nice man. We're friends to this day. He still drops in unawares when he's in the district. But a hard master, a bit of a tartar. No, that does him less than justice, he could be very frightening. While directing, he would go up to the circle and when he left the stalls we knew we were in trouble. Suddenly this great booming voice would erupt.

"Lovely hearts!" If it was "Lovely hearts", then he'd lost his temper and patience and was absolutely furious. "Lovely hearts . . . I CAN'T HEAR A WORD FROM UP

HERE!" Just hearing it in memory, tickles me. "Lovely hearts" and then all that rage, it's the marvellous incongruity.

Yet Frank, for all the sound and fury, had a soft heart. He was a sentimentalist, easily moved. His real name is Mario Francelli, he's of Italian stock. In Coronation Year he took us to Norwich for a six-week season. Coronation Day, 1953, found Frank and myself, thanks to television, in a pub, watching our young queen crowned, the pair of us in tears.

When I'd been with him for about a year, Frank started the Oxford Playhouse School of Drama. It was a bit of a come-on really, not exactly a recognised and official academy, but harmless enough. Senior members of the cast held classes for young hopefuls, a dozen to fifteen of them, the majority girls. One part-time student, Jean Wagstaff, became The Girlfriend and then The Fiancée, though it petered out when I went to London and she married a professional footballer, I believe.

The school reminds me of my dire track record as talent spotter. It's boring and tiresome of me, no doubt, but I have always believed in keeping unhelpful opinions to myself. There is enough of that around, I'm not causing a world shortage or anything. So personal criticism is avoided if possible. But I have advised two people to give up the stage . . . and both went on to be roaring successes.

The first to be warned off was Ian and Alastair Smith's kid sister Margaret. They were the twins who'd been at the architectural school, and I knew Margaret through them. Understudying the leading character man meant filling in for him at Playhouse acting classes as well. There were plentiful chances to study Margaret, who was an assistant stage manager and getting experience on stage. We appeared together in the school comedy, *Housemaster*. She was reported as having given "a racy performance" but I didn't rate her. To my mind Margaret had only two styles, either grand and rather camp, or sharp Cockney. No matter what the role, she seemed to make it one or the other.

Nothing wrong with that, Cary Grant got away with it for years. Some performers, unwittingly or otherwise, play themselves. Some want to become different people, on stage.

All the same, poor little Margaret didn't impress me. I'd look at her and think, "*Uh-oh, you are not going to make it, dear.*"

Very well, time passed, both of us had moved on to London, and I ran into Margaret, we started chatting and she unburdened herself. "I'm not getting any work, what d'you think I should do, Ronnie? I don't know what to do, whether to carry on."

As gently as possible, I said, "If I were you, Margaret, I'd give it up."

She gave me a funny look and said, "Oh, would you?" For some reason she wasn't the least grateful for my wisdom. And she didn't take my advice, the fool.

Maggie Smith, idol of the theatre and rightfully so, Oscar winner for *The Prime of Miss Jean Brodie* and *California Suite*!

David Warner is the only other colleague I have ever told to forget it, find a more promising profession, and *he* hasn't done badly, either. We'll come to that in its place; meanwhile, you may take it that getting warned off by me is an infallible omen of huge success.

Working in my home town had its cosy side. I was living with my parents and going to work on the bus; I even cycled there occasionally. It was a lovely time both sides of the footlights. We could get to matinees at Oxford's other theatre, the New, for everything from variety with the likes of Fred Emney, to musicals of the day. I saw university stagings of the classics, such as Professor Nevill Coghill's memorable *A Midsummer Night's Dream*, and he signed a pass, still in my possession, getting me in to a lecture by John Gielgud at the Sheldonian.

81

Oxford was so beautiful then, too. They've cut the heart out of it since, one wonders how they dared. Put a fence around the High, the Radcliffe Camera and Magdalen Bridge, and that would be the Oxford of my youth, give or take a few more unspoilt areas of the city.

Professionally, the roles were diverse. We did *Rebecca* – game girl, notice how she keeps cropping up? At Bramhall, Glenn Melvyn played Maxim and I'd had a good part as well. Now I was told I had to be the butler, and didn't I resent it! Thought myself worthy of something better than the rotten old butler.

By way of consolation I did get to be Danny in *Night Must Fall*, the role which had captured my imagination as a teenager with the amateur drama group. Strictly speaking I was fifty per cent of Danny, a riddle explained by Frank Shelley's brainstorm – my friend John Randall would be leading man the first week, with me as Danny the second. Frank must have hoped that people would see the same play twice to compare interpretations. Not an original gimmick, by the way. It was done at the London Old Vic before World War Two, though with slightly more eminent actors, the likes of Olivier, Redgrave and Gielgud alternating in Shakespeare productions.

And there were other leads for me. I played Agatha Christie's 'little grey cells' sleuth, Poirot, in what amounted to a trilogy at the Playhouse, over some months – *Black Coffee*, *Peril at End House* and *Alibi*. Mrs Christie describes him most clearly and precisely: bald, just a streak of hair on top, and the lovingly-cultivated moustache. A contemporary photo shows that I managed the look; it wasn't flattering but unlike many stage and screen Poirots, facially it *was* him!

All three plays are whodunits, escapist entertainment, which doesn't prevent them being quite challenging. In some ways *Alibi* is more demanding, and with a greater number of speeches, than *Hamlet*: Poirot is discovered when the curtain goes up on Act One and stays there until the final curtain. It's a test of memory and concentration, never mind the acting, because the wretched man keeps asking questions and, being in a whodunit, they affect the plot and have to be got right, not to mention in the right order. More than five hundred of them. You can't paraphrase – parrot-face, we used to call that – too boldly. "I put it to you . . ." instead of "Is it not true that . . ." is about the limit.

Very wearing, to keep some six hundred and sixty speeches in your head, the majority of them being questions. Paul Daniels with his memory test has nothing on that!

By the completion of the trilogy I'd rather gone off detective drama. Imagine my feelings when the next production to be announced was a Christie play, *The Hollow*.

"Don't, please don't make me be Poirot again, Frank," I pleaded.

Frank Shelley treated me to his faintly enigmatic smile and said, "He isn't in *The Hollow*, you blockhead." Then he cast me as the Detective Inspector!

"Played with an air of faint depression", a local drama critic decided, and no wonder.

I even got into uniform at the Playhouse. If you've been wondering why I wasn't wearing it for at least two years in real life, National Service being the rule in the 'fifties, I should explain that as well as the boyhood nephritis which nearly killed me, I had an operation for a tubercular gland when I was about fifteen. Apart from being the start of well-roundedness (I think being made to drink a lot of milk started a lifelong weight problem – I began dieting at Bramhall) it didn't affect me. But when I took my National Service medical, they told me to wait until there was a Third World War, when they might conscript me.

This didn't break my heart, I'd have resented two years in the Services when I was mad to be an actor. I joined the army, all the same, for *Carrington VC* at Oxford. Frank got the Royal Army Ordnance Corps, which had a major depot at Didcot, to send officers to check our appearance and bearing and generally coach us.

Whatever else it might have been, Frank Shelley's programme at the Playhouse was varied. *Saloon Bar* (Billie Whitelaw did her homework at the Gloucester Arms, five yards from the stage door, learning to pull pints before playing the barmaid) and *Charlie's Aunt*, to Anouilh's version of the Orpheus and Eurydice legend, *Point of Departure*, which gave me my first leading role, as Orphée. There was Poirot, and *The Lady's Not For Burning*.

While doing a lot of comedy, I didn't see myself as a specialist. And serious or jolly, lightweight or solemn, it was a wonderful way to earn a living. Not having knowledge of the Playhouse's financial picture – it always seemed to be doing fine, from my selfish point of view, appearing in play after play – there seemed no reason for things not going on this way.

But there were major changes in the offing.

11

A BRAZENLY NAKED LIGHT

OXFORD was fine, I was almost into a rut there, enjoying the big fish – well, largish – in small pond syndrome. Nice things were said about me in the local press. The run as Poirot and several more good parts had won me a bit of a following, it was all very pleasant. But the company was in financial difficulties and sold out to the London Mask Theatre, run by a man with the wonderfully theatrical name of Thane Parker. He took over at Oxford with Hugh Goldie as director and an entire young touring company which had been doing Shakespeare.

Most of the original Playhouse team left to make way for them but Derek Francis and I were asked to stay on. We heard that Peter Hall, then a relative newcomer who'd just done something in London, would join us as a resident director. Peter Hall was fresh, full of ideas, energy, enthusiasm, and luckily for me, we took to each other.

He did three or four productions, including an olde tyme music hall entertainment. "You'll be the Chairman," he decided. That was interesting, as they say. It would be my first straight to audience thing and that meant ad-libbing. Frankly the prospect was terrifying. I had a few little ideas ready, just in case, but was ready to be found out and prove a disaster. In the event it was great fun . . . and terrifying.

Peter Hall, in a kind of Mephisto makeup, played the

piano for us and one of the ASMs, a girl called Eileen Atkins, turned his music. (I thought she had the makings, so I didn't tell *her* to give up the business. Just as well; there would come a time when I played Bottom to her Titania, for BBC television.) Margaret Smith had a number in the show.

Music hall was an eye-opener, I got the bug – enjoying the freedom of talking to the audience, the different feel of this kind of comedy. Of course all the undergraduates turned up, they loved the idea of barracking the Chairman. Foreseeing that was what had made me wary about the job. Ad-libbing was new to me.

There was a candle on my table, as I introduced each act and delivered linking patter. One of the undergraduates shouted, "What does the Lord Chamberlain say about that naked light on the stage?" (Perhaps younger readers need reminding that in those days the Lord Chamberlain was ultimate theatrical censor, scourge of nudity.)

Good joke, even if the lad had been sitting there getting it ready . . . But what *did* the Lord Chamberlain have to say? I opened my mouth, wondering, and heard myself saying, "That's not a naked light, sir, it's fully covered by our insurance policy." Everybody cheered.

Peter Hall told me off for saying "Jolly good," all the time. There was an answer for that, too. "It's not repetitive," I said loftily, "it's a catchphrase!"

My last play at Oxford, *Listen To The Wind*, was with Peter. Another fun thing, I played a mad gipsy who hated bread and butter and had a special song about it. One evening during the run, a drunken electrician we had came stumbling up the stairs to my dressing room and mumbled, "Alastair Sim's waiting to see you."

Now Alastair Sim was among my idols and exemplars, had been for years. He wouldn't be hanging around the stage door to see me. However, the Smith twins, Alastair and Ian, often dropped in to the Playhouse, so the explanation was obvious. "You mean Alastair *Smith*," I said, and Sparks mumbled, "Right you are," or whatever and went back downstairs.

Sure enough, Alastair Smith was there when I went out. "What d'you want?" I asked him. He looked surprised. No, he'd sent no message, he was here to walk his sister Margaret home. Neither of us could understand it. Until out of the shadows materialised this large, looming, caped figure. "Good evening . . . my name is Alastair Sim." He *had* been waiting while I took my time removing the makeup and fiddling about!

"I'm doing a play in London," said Sim, "and I'd like you to come and do a part in it."

My heart sank, I couldn't believe it. What should have been a thrilling offer really upset me. Because I had to turn him down.

Glenn Melvyn, yet again, was involved in that. He had written *Hot Water* as a vehicle for Arthur Askey and himself. He would be Arthur's pal, with a tuh-terrible stutter and being Glenn, that stutter was beautifully observed, a work of art. Analyse it, as one had to, and there was a lot more to it than was understood by a laughing audience, terrific facial expressions blended to the sounds.

For the try-out tour, Glenn asked me to play the friend while he did the Askey role. That's where Arkwright got his trademark . . . Obviously a fairly long tour in what was bound to be a success, especially with a friend like Glenn, was too good an offer to refuse.

So I was committed, and had to tell Alastair Sim that I couldn't accept his offer. "Shame," he murmured, already moving away, melting back into the shadows. "I thoroughly enjoyed your performance tonight, I'd have loved you to have done it."

And then he wasn't there any more. Extraordinary man, magnetic, a sort of Svengali personality and, at the same time, very private and self-contained. Though frustrating, getting a job-offer from Sim was a truly memorable event of my spell at Oxford.

The sequel was that I saw him long afterwards in the
BBC canteen at Acton. Never having seen myself as a
star, whatever that is, I've always been starstruck and
rather in awe of performers whom one admires without
knowing as private individuals. So I felt unable to go
over and introduce myself, but Alastair Sim buttonholed
me as I went out. Plainly he'd forgotten our previous
meeting.

"You're my favourite," he confided, "wonderfully
funny." Turning it into a back-handed compliment by
adding thoughtfully, "Yes, you're really my favourite on
television . . . you and the Goodies."

Returning to the 1950s and the Oxford Playhouse,
the very end of my time there proved that it was the
springboard to the West End. Suddenly the chances
were there. An offer from Alastair Sim, no less, and
Peter Hall invited me to make my London debut in
his production of *Mourning Becomes Electra* at the Arts
Theatre Club.

I could accept, since Glenn Melvyn's tour would be
over in a couple of months, before Peter's production
went into rehearsal.

"Don't get blasé . . ." Well, we would see.

12

THE CHAMP CALLED AGNES

OUT of *Hot Water*, Northern farce written with Arthur Askey in mind, and into *Mourning Becomes Electra*, one couldn't complain of lack of variety. Peter Hall's 1955 revival of Eugene O'Neill's grotesquely long play, three plays in one really, gave me my start in the West End at the Arts Theatre Club. A national newspaper reviewer, having said that O'Neill was greatly overrated, claimed that *Mourning* "runs four hours and feels like eight".

That's grossly unfair and misleading – it ran for five and three-quarter hours. An audience for the seven p.m. performance had to be kept waiting the best part of an hour for the matinee to finish! (And the evening audience wouldn't get out until the early hours of the following day.)

Mary Morris rebelled when it was planned to solve that problem by starting matinees at lunchtime. She refused to do a matinee at all; in the play throughout, two performances would have kept her on stage for more than eleven hours. Some of us were luckier, I was in the second and third plays of the trilogy, others a single one. You'd meet people going home, as you arrived for work. "See you tomorrow." – "Yes, good-night." Rather like belonging to the same club and having acquaintances who dropped in.

We all got through it, and for the next three years I worked mainly for Peter Hall. An exception was appearing in *Double Image*, presented by Laurence Olivier and Vivien Leigh. Zena Dare was in the cast and celebrated her seventieth birthday during the run. The Oliviers threw a party for her on stage after the performance. That was the Savoy Theatre in 1957, and Vivien Leigh, so beautiful, came in to arrange flowers around the set, once the curtain had fallen.

Double Image was an ingenious thriller with Richard Attenborough playing his own twin brother. I'd been given a release to do *Camino Real*, the Tennessee Williams play which Peter Hall was directing. Richard introduced me to Olivier at the Zena Dare party, mentioning that I would be leaving to join the Peter Hall production.

"Swine – have some more champagne," said Olivier.

Charm, friendliness, style, and all in five words. One of the few regrets of my career is that I never worked with him. The pay wouldn't have needed to be high . . . but I'd have shelled out every penny I could afford! When I met my wife Joy I discovered Laurence Olivier was her idol too. She and her cousin Betty used to stand outside his Chelsea home for hours, hoping for a glimpse of him, when they were girls. Our first child is named Laurence after Olivier.

That was what made it such a thrill for us when we met Lord Olivier at the British Academy of Film and Television Arts annual awards, about ten years ago.

I was there to receive an award; somebody tapped my shoulder and it was Olivier. "I just wanted to say that I've always admired you" – *he'd* admired *me* – "and your performances are wonderful." And he sat down and the three of us talked for three-quarters of an hour, a happily memorable evening for Joy and me.

But back to Peter Hall. He had a taste for the unusual, and Tennessee Williams's *Camino Real* was that, certainly. Another extraordinary play with a mixture of historical and fictional characters – Don Quixote, the Lady of the Camellias, Baron de Charlus, Casanova . . .

A big cast, naturally, many of whom I was to work

with again. Liz Seal, Denholm Elliott, decades away from bed, breakfast and fleas with those Spanish monks, many more. Harry Andrews played Casanova, Diana Wynyard was Marguerite Gautier, Robert Hardy was Byron.

I had three roles, including Sancho Panza to John Wood's Quixote, and Nursie, a transvestite bouncer in a brothel. Les Girls included an actress by the name of Bandana Das Gupta! Wonderful piece, very weird – *Camino Real*, that is.

Before that, Peter staged Ugo Betti's *Summertime*. It's a slight, charming little play about romantic misunderstandings and young love during an Italian family's outings in the mountains. I played a peasant farmer – bandana round the head (not Ms. Das Gupta's) and beaming smile displaying a missing front tooth.

Dirk Bogarde and Geraldine McEwan were the leads. Then as now Dirk was a big film star and this was his return to the stage, guaranteeing publicity for the production. Not to mention success, it ran for about five months.

The star but not The Star, Dirk was lovely, a nice man and a kind one. For a year or so I had been collecting books, for the pictures really. At rehearsal one morning I happened to have a copy of *Dr Syntax* with the Rowlandson illustrations. Dirk noticed it and made some remark, and I said that I was going to sell it. "Don't you like it?" he asked.

"I love it," I admitted, "but I need the money and I might get a fiver for this."

"Oh, money," he said, diving into his pocket, and passed me a five-pound note. "Pay me back on the first night." That got me through the following week and I was able to keep the book.

Then I got a sub on my salary, tapped on his dressing room door and tried to pay him back. Dirk wouldn't hear of it.

"Wouldn't dream of taking it," he said, as if I were

trying to press a gift on him. "Don't be silly, Ronnie, clear off." In fact he didn't quite say clear off but it was an expletive to that effect.

It wasn't just me, he was kind and showed thoughtfulness towards everybody, a true professional and easy to work with. This is not the stuff of bestsellers but I have to say that there are any amount of thoroughly nice people in the business.

We took *Summertime* on tour to Manchester and Glasgow, before bringing it in to the Apollo in London. The tour was a reminder that, unpretentious he might be, but Bogarde was a really big star. The fan hysteria wasn't hyped, they really were carried away by the chance to see him in person. In Scotland, hundreds of youngsters jostled outside the stage door, beneath his dressing room window. And they were all chanting, *"We want – Dirk B'gard . . . We want – Dirk B'gard."*

I never forgot that, the frenzied chanting, and the Scottish accent making it very easy for Sassenachs to hear something rather different to 'Bogarde'. It made poor Dirk look a bit thoughtful, until he caught on!

His first-night telegram to me ran, "Good luck – keep that pitchfork blunt." There was a scene where I chased him round the stage with it.

The Arts Theatre had loaned Peter Hall to do the play with Dirk Bogarde, and once it was running in the West End he went back there to work on their Christmas show, *Listen To The Wind.*

That was the one we'd done at Oxford, when my gipsy who detested bread and butter had won Alastair Sim's approval. "Pity you can't do it again," said Peter, and that gave me an idea.

At first he assumed it was a joke. "You can't be in two places at once, Ronnie." But I could, proving it by doing twenty-two performances in two different plays in the same week. The Arts Theatre and the Apollo weren't that far apart, and *Summertime* involved me in just the last act.

Being an enthusiast/amateur, interested in every facet of the theatre was useful. The clincher for Peter Hall, when he was uncertain whether to let me try, was my pointing out that it *had* been done before, by a certain D. A. Clarke-Smith in 1935!

That went on for some six weeks – it'd kill me, now. I devised a kind of composite makeup between ruddy-cheeked Italian peasant and swarthy gipsy. This allowed me to unwrap my peasant's bandana, remove the side-burns and unblacken the 'missing' front tooth, don a big moustache for the gipsy, and be ready.

At first I commuted by taxi but found that doing it on foot was quicker and didn't put me at the mercy of traffic jams. I got some curious glances, hurrying through back-doubles on the fringe of Soho, a cross between peasant and gipsy! And being in two places at once, not to mention two plays, brought combined pay of £27, with the Arts Theatre paying £12 of it.

Whether working there or not, I spent a lot of time in the Arts Theatre Club's snack bar, that's where you met your friends. All the 'resting' actors turned up there, it was a recognised place for picking up gossip, work, and generally proving that one was still around.

Another Ronnie, Ronnie Curtis, a casting director for cheap films, found a lot of his people there. His office was just round the corner, so it was handy for him. There'd be a stir when he came in. It was quite common for, say, Sean Connery, Michael Caine and Ian Hendry to be making their cups of coffee last – the Arts snack bar didn't serve alcohol – in order to get up and start looking macho and magnetic for Ronnie Curtis.

The thing was, he had this terrible squint. He'd tip the wink to someone, and the chap sitting next to him would ask, "Who, me?" hopefully, only for Ronnie to point to a third fellow, unsuspected until then, and say, "No, you over there!"

Eventually I was the one 'over there' in the snack bar. Ronnie got me one day's work at £7 a day on something called *Sailor of Fortune* – unfortunate title, these days. Now this was an exciting event, a personal milestone, I was going to be in a real film!

Anticlimactically after that build-up, I remember nothing about it really, beyond travelling out to some Home Counties location on the train and being very thrilled. When it came to my bit, Lorne Greene the star of the TV Western *Bonanza* was being very butch but wasn't wearing Stetson and spurs, so it must have been a thriller. I played a waiter who cowered behind a table and got shot at; I may even have been shot.

The Buckstone Club was another regular haunt, where I met Ronnie Corbett, and which led to meeting my wife, Joy. The Buckstone was in a basement in a street leading up from the Strand, over there behind the Haymarket. It was a stage people's place, with different clientele according to the time of day.

In the afternoons luminaries were found there. It was convenient for many theatres, after the matinee or between shows. "Sir John and Sir Ralph sitting over poached eggs and a pot of tea," as Ronnie C. remembers the scene. Later at night, the luminaries weren't there. I expect they had homes to go to, and preserved their sanctity or sanity . . . whatever it was they were intent on preserving.

That cleared the stage for younger and less careful folk. We stayed until four in the morning sometimes. In fairness, a session might start when your show was over, so the evening was just beginning when nine-to-five folk were tucked up in bed. It may have been against regulations and breached legal opening hours but nothing desperate went on, just social drinking and chat, unwinding. No offence was caused.

I first met Ronnie Corbett at the Buckstone, over a drink. Well, I was over it and he was under it. A voice came out of thin air and I thought it was the drink talking, until something made me peer over the other side of the bar – and there he was. He had boxes to stand

94

on, one marked AGNES and the other, CHAMP. It took a while to work out that they were champagne boxes cut in half . . .

Back to reality. Ronnie knew the club's owners so he was in there a lot, either working behind the bar or drinking on the customers' side. It was a bit confusing. We got to know each other casually, nodding terms, exchange greetings, pass the time of day. We weren't bosom pals or anything; it was that quite common relationship, a chap you know from the pub.

Certainly we made no plans to work together, then. If it happened, well and good. But for a number of years yet, I would see the Buckstone not as the club where I met Ronnie C., but the start of the road towards the best thing that ever happened to me – marrying Joy.

13

JOY

WALKING into the theatre that first morning, I was
greeted by a vintage comic postcard situation, begging
for a caption. She was stage manager, wearing cotton
trousers, very tight, and bending over a property basket
or something. "I know that face!" I said.

My future wife captured my attention before she
turned around . . .

Tony Knowles, who ran the Buckstone Club, also put
on shows. He'd set up out-of-town productions for short
seasons, on a modest budget, and they tended to do
well. Towards the end of 1956 he invited me to take
part in his latest project, a double bill to be staged at
Cambridge for three weeks.

The plays were Somerset Maugham's *The Letter*, and
the Wolf Mankowitz four-hander, *The Bespoke Overcoat*.
My mother had moved to Cambridge and the prospect
of seeing something of her made it a pleasant little
engagement.

Joy claims that she didn't hear my joke at her expense,
which was just as well – though she's heard it often
enough since! We were introduced, and my bachelor
days were numbered. The first impression was of viv-
acity, energy and a nice nature. She had dark hair then
– blonde now, courtesy of the hairdresser – wonderful
smile, wonderful laugh. (You heard it on all *The Two
Ronnies*.)

Aged three — I have never looked more angelic, even when I played in *My Three Angels* at Cheltenham.

Right: The one that featured in the photographer's shop window. This, I suppose, could be called my first public appearance.

The school photo, 1938, at Donnington Junior School, Oxford. Glasses, my subsequent trade-mark, appear for the first time.

My grandfather and sister Vera in the back yard of the Victorian terraced house in Bedford, 1933. I've played many characters that look like him since then.

Getting plumper, after my hospital stint. The supercilious look was in reality uncertainty as to where to look. In later years it was "Which camera are we on?".

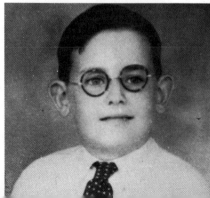

Playing the sixteen-year-old spiv.

Above right: With the Mime Theatre Company in 1950 (obviously sub-Errol Flynn).

Right: The two of us in 1957. I married my one and only Joy.

Below Right: At the Playhouse, Oxford, I was required to play juvenile parts. This must have been one of them!

Below: My early impression of Bob Monkhouse, about 1958.

The family man, reading to baby
Charlotte from an old nursery
book.

My complete brood, in the pool in
Sydney, Australia, 1979.

Domestic bliss in the garden. I can't believe the joke I've just quoted from
the script was as funny as that, but all my family became good actors for
the camera.

A pageful of *Porridge*, with Fulton McKay and my late and much lamented friend, Richard Beckinsale. This was without doubt the pinnacle of my career.

Big Jim Jehosaphat and Fat-Belly Jones. These hairy folk-singers ran through six series of *The Two Ronnies*. I loved writing the numbers for the daft pair.

The Japanese No-No Theatre. RB: "I play mighty oaks and forests!".
RC: I play bushes and bonsai trees".

Representing the Raj, singing Noel
Coward's 'Mad Dogs and
Englishmen'.

The Drum Majorettes. I can still
feel the corset that Mary Husband,
our superb costume designer,
squeezed me in to. She did most
splendid work for us over the
years.

Sid and George, I think perhaps the public's favourite *Two Ronnies* characters.

Saturday Night Fervour, c 1982.

As a couple of Vicarious Vikings, Mudgard the Mighty and Pith the Pathetic.

The mainstay of my career and family life Joy, my wife and dearest friend.
I still have a postcard which I was sent one birthday:
"Health and love around you stay,
And joy go with you all the way."
That will do me fine.

The theatrical tradition in our family comes from Joy. Her grandmother, stagestruck, wanted all her daughters on the stage. Joy's mother dug her heels in but her sister, Joy's Auntie Mabs, became a Tiller Girl, went on to Paris and the Folies Bergère and understudied Mistinguett. Mabs married a variety performer and, even after he retired, they worked for Arthur Lucan, famous as Old Mother Riley.

So Joy grew up with theatre talk and an interest in the profession. World War Two put paid to her ambition to be a chorus girl. Her first job was with the Rank Organisation, secretary in the division running all the Odeon cinemas. It had just one live theatre, at Bromley, Kent. Joy was in the firm's amateur drama club, and when a vacancy came up at the New Theatre, Bromley, a colleague looking after the accounts there got Joy the job.

It was rather like my experience with Frank Shelley at Oxford. She got taken on as a student at £2 a week, a big drop from her previous pay. There was a family conference and they agreed to help out. Even so, Joy must have been dedicated, because working at the New Theatre meant travelling right across London, then a train to Bromley, daily.

Then, when Joy arrived for her first day, the manager said he couldn't afford to pay her anything. Joy's mother, terrific lady, said, "Take the job anyway, we'll manage." Joy made herself indispensable and the result was that in less than a month they started paying her.

She joined the New in 1953, as a dogsbody, and by the time we met three years later, was a fully-fledged stage manager. And an excellent one, too. Much chopped liver had to be eaten during *The Bespoke Overcoat* and I loathe the stuff, it nauseates me. So on top of everything else, Joy used to go home every night and make a very stiff chocolate blancmange for me to eat instead. On stage, it looked acceptable. When we were married, Joy promised to make me a nice chocolate

97

blancmange and I had to confess that the *other* dish I detested was just that. She was speechless! But how could I have rejected the substitute, when she was going to so much trouble to make it for me?

Chocolate blancmange apart, Joy and I were on the same wavelength from the start, though she was seeing another actor at Cambridge called Martin. I set about altering that! She'd be sitting by the prompt book at rehearsals and the more I saw of her, the more I liked her. Playing the Chinaman, I had to be in an opium den scene, and as stage manager, she gave me the pipe. I did this little gag of inhaling from it, coughing and choking, then shooting her a reproachful glance, offstage.

Maybe I'm a chauvinist, though unsure what it means. Women should be in their place but that place is everywhere. My great favourite, Fred Emney, used to love sending ladies up, and I thought it funny and lovable, it made them like you. It worked with Joy. The pipe business made her fall about and from that moment – she told me later – Joy decided I was a lot of fun.

A party, including my rival Martin, went punting on the Cam and Joy invited me along. And though he was there, she sat by me. A hopeful sign, surely, and I was in with a chance.

All love stories are unique and identical. It was great to be alive and seeing Joy. The old songs are right, it was a lovely time when emotions and senses were heightened, everything looked brighter and clearer, one noticed flowers and heard birds singing. Even before meeting, we had liked the same people. Laurence Olivier, of course, Paul Mayo, a designer whom Joy admired at Bromley, had been with me at the Oxford Playhouse. So had Francis Matthews, talented actor famous as television's Paul Temple in the 1960s. And Joy worked with Ronnie Corbett before I did. He'd done pantomime at Bromley and from up on the lighting grid, she watched his entrance as Mummy Bear, drawn in on a sledge!

By the time the play opened we were close enough to share private jokes, laugh at the same things. And as it happened, there were reasons for laughter, that evening. The leading man in *The Letter* had just been offered work in New York, so he was full of that, spending no end of time on the phone to his agent. Suddenly three weeks at Cambridge wasn't the biggest thing on his mind. The curtain went up on *The Letter*, and the leading man wasn't there. He'd gone off somewhere (another phone call?) and missed his entrance.

I wasn't on yet, just standing beside Joy in the wings, watching it all unfolding. Or unravelling. There was nothing the people on stage could do, except talk among themselves for a while until he managed to turn up.

As you'd expect, mild chaos set in. James Ottaway, playing the solicitor, a character called Joyce, made his entrance and announced himself. Unfortunately, he happened to have his hand on his hip when he told the audience, "I'm Joyce."

It got the appropriate reaction and, terribly shaken, poor James told the leading lady to pull herself together, which was his next line. Only he didn't quite say that. With great sternness and authority he ordered, "Pull yourself to pieces."

By which time Joy and I were helpless, biting the laughter back. I think that was our first awareness of affinity, of being in something together and knowing exactly how the other person was feeling. A hilarious occasion, it was also an important one for us.

Part way through the run, I found that we'd been out together three or four times. "What are you doing tonight?" had become, "Where are we going after the show?" The snag being that I was about to go into *Double Image* in the West End while Joy was set to leave Cambridge and go on tour as stage manager with another play, *The Trial of Mary Dugan*. And after that, *The Caine Mutiny*, with its all-male cast . . . I didn't approve of that at all!

Yes, there was no reason for it but I was a little bit jealous, or worried that I might lose her while we were apart, anyway. I shouldn't have worried, because we'd fallen for each other. Of course once her tour finished we got together again, we'd meet at the Arts Theatre snack bar. But it was in the restaurant of the Royal Court Theatre, Sloane Square, that I proposed to her. Some people have two wedding ceremonies but we had two proposals.

At the Royal Court, I'd had a few and might have been a bit sloshed, though that had nothing to do with it. I asked Joy to be my wife and she agreed.

Next day, she asked, "Remember what you asked me last night, Ronnie?"

Of course I did.

"Well, I *still* will," said Joy. And we got married soon afterwards, on 8 July 1957. We were absolutely flat broke, she had no money, I had none. So it was a tiny wedding and a tiny reception – ham and lettuce in a restaurant at Stanmore and we lived at my flat, also tiny, in Hampstead Hill Gardens.

Everything I want to tell you about Joy can be summed up by saying that she well deserves her name.

I thought I loved her when we got married; well, I knew I did, that's why you ask somebody to marry you. More often than not, anyway. But I didn't know the half of it. It has just got better, deeper, year by year. Along with our children, she is the most important thing in my life, improving and giving purpose to every part of it.

Joy really runs things at home. Giving up her career was a wrench but adjustment was easier because she could identify with what I was doing. We are complementary, and speak the same language. When I grumbled that a director wanted me to move upstage when it should be down, she knew what it meant. She says that if she'd married a stockbroker, for instance, she would have been completely cut off – he would not have known what she was talking about. With me, Joy stayed in the same environment and kept in touch with what she'd left behind.

Joy typed all my scripts and I valued her advice. She would tell me if a certain sketch was too clever – it's not big-headedness to worry over being too clever, the most sophisticated audience needs time to assimilate an idea – and when I heard her laughing as she typed, then the omens were favourable!

Her theory, and I agree with it, is that there are two kinds of humour, something you laugh at once, because it's new, and another category which is amusing every time you hear it. She has listened to Ronnie C.'s warm-up routine for years, and certain bits always break her up. *"He was a very interesting man when he was alive . . . after he died he got a bit ordinary,"* for example.

Some of Ronnie's gems have gone into our family repertoire, they're a part of conversation like any other quotation. *"Are you mad or have you been drinking the bitter? "* is a standby.

Nobody could ask for a better or more loyal and supportive partner than Joy. All she wanted was for us to be happy and the children to be all right – she has never been demanding, ambitious, any of that. Not all that long after we got married there was a moment when she wondered what on earth she'd got into – I was just a young, not particularly well known, jobbing actor and my career could have gone in any direction, including straight down – but it was a passing thought.

The marvellous thing about Joy, one of the marvellous things, is her sincere belief that something will turn up and things will turn out all right, somehow. "You never know what's hanging until it drops," was her mother's watchword, and that attitude saw us through crises.

It would be silly to claim that we have never had rows. Joy went through a terrible bout of depression after the birth of our daughter, Charlotte in 1962. It was a trau-matic period, we nearly came to blows . . . to be honest, *we* didn't but I nearly struck her, out of frustration and panic that things would never be the same again.

But she recovered, thank God, and we got on with our lives.

Before my marriage I was fast and loose as any young fellow. I started young, too – though not by today's standards – at Aylesbury. Remember the seven girl students, four friendly and three not, or possibly vice-versa? Well, one of the four or three was friendliest and this pale, virginal, well-brought-up girl caught us cuddling on the hearthrug one evening and was *disgusted*. Within a week or two, she became The Girlfriend!

I was engaged twice, to Jean Wagstaff and a girl called Vivienne Barnard. That was an unofficial engagement, an understanding, but it lasted eighteen months and might have come to something. Her father was a Brigadier and didn't approve of me, parental discouragement wore Vivienne down, she hated deceiving her father and seeing me after promising not to, so that faded away. Jean Wagstaff's father was less than ecstatic, for that matter; there were strong hints that I should get a proper job, preferably working in his shop . . .

Actors, certainly young and unproven ones, risked being regarded as rogues and vagabonds, in the 1950s. Possibly that hasn't changed!

I took those engagements seriously though, there was none of the American attitude of let's-get-engaged-and-work-out-the-divorce-later. But there were lots of girls between times, not necessarily steamy, sexy affairs, it was all very carefree and lighthearted.

Some readers may nod sceptically, reflecting that I would say that, downplaying an enjoyably active social life! But I wasn't a matinee idol, rather too well-rounded to cut a romantic figure. Ronnie Barker, alias The Stud? Hardly. We weren't pop stars, there were no groupies.

As for actresses, it was a swings and roundabouts thing. There were plenty of extremely attractive girls who made the best of themselves and usually were a long way from home and therefore parental control – a rare event, forty years ago. But they knew the score, not to mention knowing how to look after themselves, and couldn't be conned.

Marriage to Joy kept me away from the swings *and* the roundabouts. Showbusiness is full of temptations and I have been physically tempted, no normal man could fail to be. But it has always been fleeting; I have too much to lose.

Joy is worth so much more to me than a temporary affaire.

I just love her too much, she is my lodestone and foundation. If she left me, for whatever reason, I think I would pine away, like a dog.

14

MAKE ME LAUGH

PEOPLE can be touchy, there are libel laws, one must have a care. On the other hand I am allowed to hold opinions, they can't touch you for that. On which note, it should be pointed out that Peter Brook is an eminent man of the theatre, one of those names springing to mind when directors are discussed. His first production was in 1952, the list takes up inches in *Who's Who*. And in my opinion he was never the director he was built up to be. He didn't seem practical to me, speaking from experience of the only time I worked for him. We didn't get on!

The play was *Irma La Douce*, a hit, and the year 1958. Many readers will have seen a version – there was a film as well as various stagings – and those who haven't may be aware that it's about that stock heroine the tart with a heart, Irma in this case, and a student lover who gets in all sorts of trouble when jealousy inspires him to pose in disguise as a wealthy client.

My role was fairly minor, one of four Paris gangsters, *mecs* or spivs, who befriend him. By now I'd been in London for some three years and appeared in a number of plays, many of them for Peter Hall, my Oxford Playhouse contact. It was back to smaller parts and as a newly-married man *Irma* seemed a great stroke of good fortune. Joy and I danced round the kitchen of our little

North London flat, transported over me having landed a job paying £30 a week.

Peter Brook was directing and his habit of starting rehearsals with, "What are we going to do today?" used to worry me. I would have been happier if he'd known what we were going to do; that was what he was for. No doubt he did and this was just a rhetorical flourish, but it did open the door to suggestions, even from minions like me.

Irma has an escape scene where the *mecs* overpower their island guards and escape aboard a raft, singing lustily the while, since the whole thing takes place during a number. Well, it is a musical.

Peter announced: "What we'll do here is that you rip the palisade down to build a raft, jump the guards, tear blankets into strips and tie them, build the raft, jump aboard and pole yourselves away."

"Pardon?" I thought. And out loud, "But Peter, we've only got sixteen bars for that."

"It won't take that long," he said airily, "the blankets can be pre-cut, ready."

"Have you thought about the next performance?" I asked. "Who's going to put all the blankets together again?" He'd been talking of tearing the blankets into inch-wide strips, and I had a vision of them being sewn into place, strip by strip. Mr Brook's plan was utterly impractical and my tactless hints to that effect started irking him.

"What do you suggest?" he snapped. Actually, I did have some suggestions. Instead of building individual posts into a raft – easier to say quickly than do – have an entire section of the palisade prepared, with castors on the side hidden from the audience. That way, we could pull it down and pole away with minimum delay. And there had to be ropes ready to secure the guards. That's how it was done for ensuing years of a very successful run. No great feat of imagination on my part, it was common sense.

But I got the impression that Peter Brook didn't see it in that light. He took to asking, "Well, Ronnie, what are we going to do about such-and-such?" when queries or problems arose during rehearsals. His carping got to me; it wasn't clever, any more than his standard sneer, "Ah, here's the funny man, make me laugh, then."

"I will, if I have some lines," I'd retort blandly. And I put a few in, serve him right.

"Don't get blasé," Ivor Humphris had said. But 'blasé' wasn't the word, in the end! I auditioned to get into *Irma La Douce*, was delighted to be given the part . . . and it nearly drove me mad before it was all over. Escaping from Devil's Island was a doddle compared to breaking out of that confounded play.

The company, in both senses of the word, was fine. I got on well with Keith Michell. Liz Seal, who made her name as Irma, was a darling, Gary Raymond was a mate and Clive Revill, who had an important role as the Narrator, had shared a flat with me in Hampstead.

But I have always had this instinct to quit while I'm ahead, leave the audience wanting more, and not get into a long, predictable groove. So even though I needed the money and the security guaranteed by a West End hit, I asked for a get-out clause in my contract, freeing me after a year.

The management seemed a little surprised but was sympathetic. A get-out clause could not actually be written into the contract, they explained, but if I got a good offer after being in *Irma* for twelve months or so, they would not stand in my way. Remember, we were negotiating before the play went on; the whole thing might be academic, it could flop and close down within days.

Irma La Douce, to coin a phrase, ran and ran. It began to pall on us within a year – not just me, many of the cast. However good the show or the performances, sheer familiarity wears you down, eroding commitment and concentration. And fourteen months into the marathon, I was offered the part of Sweeny Todd in a new musical.

Not the Sondheim version, another one being mooted in the 1950s.

I went to the management and asked for my release, as promised. But they said there must have been some misunderstanding. No such agreement was in the contract, I'd got it wrong, my memory was at fault, nothing had been said about letting me go.

Naturally I was frustrated, disillusioned, furious. Word got around, and it emerged that many of the cast had laboured under an identical misunderstanding! Poor Julian Orchard finished up doing four and a quarter years.

I'm pretty sure that this situation led Equity, the theatre union, to bring in its rule forbidding managements to lock performers into productions, get-out clauses which may be invoked after a reasonable time, are mandatory.

I learnt my lesson, of course. "Get it in the contract." For ever afterwards, I did. No more gentlemen's agreements for me.

With the exception of one, of course – the agreement I had throughout my career with that most gentle of gentlemen, Peter Eade, my agent and manager. It was his policy not to have anything that would bind either party.

"If we get along, then there is no need for a contract. If we fight, then it is better we should part."

Those two very funny performers, Joan Sims and Kenneth Williams, were under his wing too, and we all respected and loved him. He died, suddenly, while I was travelling to Australia in 1979, soon after attending on my behalf the funeral of my dear old pal Richard Beckinsale, the inimitable Godber in *Porridge*, the prison series.

But to retun from a prison of which I have nothing but fond memories, to another type of prison – locked up tight in a West End run that seemed interminable. Day followed day. It drove me into a most peculiar emotional state, not suicidal but despairing, very close to a nervous breakdown. I'd be physically sick before leaving home for the theatre. There were periods when I couldn't bear the bright lights in the courtroom scene and sat there trying to pull my coat over my head. I wasn't trying to work my ticket, nor sabotage the play, it was quite unobtrusive: sliding down in the seat, turning away and drawing the lapel of my jacket farther and farther across my face. If the audience noticed – the four *mecs* were just dressing the set at that point, hardly any lines to speak – they assumed it was just a little bit of business.

Gary Raymond and I passed time by getting a large screen and covering it with a collage created from antique prints. They cost hardly anything at the time, bundles for a matter of coppers. Heaven knows where that screen ended up, but it could be worth a lot today.

There was a bright interlude. I shared a dressing room with a nice chap, David Evans, who was related to John Gielgud. After the matinee one afternoon, Gielgud put his head round the door to say hello to David and tell us he'd enjoyed the show.

"I have . . . *a little friend* outside, may I bring him in?" he asked, rather coyly.

David and I looked at each other. We couldn't refuse, though we did wonder what he meant. John Gielgud stepped aside and in walked Laurence Olivier! The god who had been responsible for my only truancy as a schoolboy, when I had to see *Henry V* all over again, was visiting my dressing room.

John Gielgud and Laurence Olivier had enjoyed *Irma La Douce* that afternoon but some of us weren't enjoying it a bit. And when actors get bored or browned-off, joking sets in, little pranks, and we're vulnerable to corpsing. That expression comes from a stage corpse smiling or even giggling, the very last thing it's supposed to do. For the moment, I'll stick to *Irma La Douce*'s corpses.

It's a broad canvas, corpsing, and embraces both the

gigglers and people setting out to provoke giggles. Unprofessional; and virtually every performer has fallen victim. Some are more at risk than others. Broadly speaking, the most solemn, unlikeliest looking people are terrible corpsers.

Under that heading comes John Neville. Serious actor, beautiful looking man, a matinee idol. You'd think butter wouldn't melt in his mouth. Not so. He joined *Irma* after a year of my sentence, and soon set about brightening up that courtroom scene.

His challenge was for us, the four *mecs*, to copy the way he sat, a short distance away. If he crossed his legs a certain way, we must adopt the stance, and so on. Easy at first, but gradually John worked first his feet and then his long legs into weirder and weirder attitudes. In those days the manager wore a dinner jacket and from the corner of an eye one caught the gleam of the white shirtfront as he prowled in the wings. He was a martinet, so the game had to be played extremely cautiously, in moves of an inch or less at a time . . .

By the end of the scene the players would all be sitting there, as it might be with one foot at an angle of forty-five degrees, the other leg crooked way up with heel just resting on the opposite knee – ridiculous. Next night, John would have his legs twined around the chair, contorted like spaghetti.

Actors on the other side of the stage, perfectly understandably, thought this very stupid and would have no part of it. They were too adult and mature for such nonsense. And then, perhaps three weeks later, I glanced up and a chap in the adult-mature lobby was twining *his* legs around the chair, mirroring John Neville. It was spreading like some terrible disease, the entire cast was doomed!

Escape seemed impossible, until I blackmailed my way out. I'd already covered for Clive Revill when he took a fortnight's holiday. Playing the narrator meant an extra £15 a week, no mean sum then, and above all it was a blessed relief with a different part, and a better one. Some months later Donald Albery arranged to open in New York, and Clive was among cast members going there to open *Irma*.

Peter Brook asked me to take over Clive's role permanently. Seeing the opening, I said that it was a strenuous role compared to sitting around as a *mec* and since they'd locked me in until the run ended, I might as well take it easy and stay where I was. They really needed to fill Clive's slot, and the upshot was an agreement that if I did it for five or six weeks while they found a replacement, I could then leave the show.

It felt like coming out of jail. I had been pleased to reach the West End, thanks to Peter Hall. Now I was thankful to get out of that little part of it occupied by the Lyric, Shaftesbury Avenue. Two years going on eternity ago, Donald Albery had sent me a charming note, following *Irma*'s first night: "You all looked like stars in the raft scene."

Had he released me to do that musical about the Demon Barber of Fleet Street, who knows, my working life might have turned out differently. A musical or two early in my career might have set me on quite another course. Similarly, after so much television comedy, there came a time when, rightly or wrongly, I was convinced that audiences simply wouldn't accept me in straight roles, so I turned them down.

Of course, you could argue that as a relative newcomer to a workplace notorious for unemployment, I was ungrateful; didn't know when I was well off. That would be true if I had been in it for the money. Since I was not, though everyone wants adequate reward for their effort, I had to enjoy the job and be stimulated by it, to be any good.

"*Don't get blasé*," Ivor Humphris warned. Well, I hadn't – but my time as a *mec*, corpsing and all, made me wiser and warier.

110

15

THE GENTLE ART OF CORPSING

IN *The Two Ronnies,* both on television and at the Palladium, we had a piece about amateur dramatics, people getting out of their depth as they wrestled with a Noel Coward-type of play. Letting you in on a not particularly well kept-secret, professionals go astray and skid into embarrassing or very silly plights on stage. It happens more often than some of us care to admit – hilariously, though the humour tends to be more enjoyable in retrospect than it seemed at the time.

Cue for another little detour, a ramble around my personal Black Museum (no, it wasn't *that* bad really) of incidents deserving the label of 'It Wasn't All Right on the Night'.

Corpsing, as I've mentioned, comes from a stage body moving, the one thing it must not do. Very unprofessional, but sometimes it can be a compulsion. John Neville started that follow-my-leader nonsense in *Irma La Douce* and it spread across the stage.

Nothing on earth will make you laugh when the audience is laughing. You're in command, generating the fun and humour, laughter doesn't occur as long as you are making others laugh.

I corpsed when things went absolutely wrong. Or fairly wrong, taking one unawares. There were times when we had rehearsed for a week, a certain line or bit of business looked certain to rock the audience. Yet

111

when you said the line, made the move . . . nothing. I'd immediately get the giggles.

At Oxford Playhouse as a young man, I'd come off night after night with a sore tongue, it was bleeding from biting it to keep a straight face. Donald Hewlett and I were in *Youth At The Helm*, another of those school plays, the infuriating part being that there was nothing particularly amusing about the passage making the pair of us corpse.

"Do you remember Farley?" I'd ask.

To which Donald's reply was, "You mean Fairy Farley, the biggest twerp in the school." That was it: a quaint Ralph Lynn sort of line. But on the first night he said, "Furry Farley" or something strange like that, and it doomed us.

Everybody has their special face when they're about to corpse. With Donald, his chin tucks in. "Do you remember Farley?" In would go the chin, down on his shoulder, and I'd think: *"He's going, he's going . . ."* Which set me off.

We got so annoyed. "Donald, I don't want to laugh."

"Quite right, neither do I."

We'd agree, nightly, that it was the wrong point in the script for a laugh, the scene was being distorted, the rest of the play might be affected, and vowed to put a stop to the corpsing. It didn't make a scrap of difference!

Random Harvest, which at Bramhall had inspired Glenn Melvyn to try greying-up a butterfly, was my undoing at Oxford, too. I had the role of the lawyer, Trustlove, and being very keen on makeup, worked out a complex succession of six or seven changes, letting me graduate subtly from maturity to old age. Though no longer stage manager, as I had been at the Tudor Theatre, I didn't have a lot of time to spare for changing.

One was especially quick – I rushed off, put a moustache on, rushed back, grabbing up my prop, a bunch of violets, and entered. Francis Matthews's stunned expression set off my alarm signals. His face was a study. Horrified, I realised that I'd made my change a scene too soon. The family lawyer had gone out to the garden for three minutes, picked the posy and returned . . . a quarter-century older.

Desperate to counteract that, I started playing the character as a juvenile – it was an impossible situation, the stuff of corpsing.

Boredom can do it as well. We did the Agatha Christie thriller with a nursery rhyme title, *Ten Little Niggers* in those insensitive days of the 'fifties. Later it became *Ten Little Indians* (I often wondered why Indians weren't supposed to mind) and finished under the current title of *And Then There Were None* – evidently nuns don't object!

And Then There Were None had a successful West End revival recently but while it's a cleverly plotted play the dialogue was very stilted and dated, even thirty years ago. Embarrassingly so, for those declaiming it. You probably know the plot: ten men and women, all with secrets to hide, tricked into weekending on an island where they are marooned and killed off, one by one, in accordance with the rhyme. I was Blore, a South African, and died when a bear fell on me. (Look, I didn't write the thing, I was just *in* it.)

At a certain point all ten characters were on stage together. That was dangerous, because there was hardly enough furniture to seat us all. We all had to face front, so often one couldn't see the person one was supposed to be addressing, simply delivered the line. Boring, unreal, embarrassing . . . therefore fraught with peril for corpsers.

A retired judge is among the guests, and during this ten-strong gathering he's poisoned. Everybody assumes the old chap has fallen into a doze, but he has been killed. An elderly actor played the judge, and he had a trick of *really* going to sleep. One of his lines was, "There's very little time, very little time."

My friend John Randall and I were sitting on a settee

113

and heard him say, "There is very little time, very lit –"
And it just stopped in the middle of the word; he'd
dropped off. But suddenly he must have woken, because
there came, '– tle time", taking up exactly where he'd
left off. The rest of the cast just sat there shaking, nobody
could say anything for a couple of minutes.

John Randall, who could always make me laugh and
went out of his way to prove it, devised games to help
us through. One of the murders takes place during a
blackout of about six seconds – the lights are supposed
to have been switched off at the mains – when all onstage
characters dash out in different directions. They're supposed to be reacting to the power failure, and return
almost at once.

There was a tin of biscuits in the wings, they were
props for an earlier scene. "Right," John proposed, "during the blackout, each of us takes a biscuit and eats it in
time to speak his next line."

Childish but fun – he was on. Giggling in the darkness,
we stuffed the biscuits into our mouths, pelted back to
the settee, and the lights went on. Good game, you had
to dispose of the biscuit gradually, without giving the
game away to the audience, but fast enough to be ready
for speech. The handicap was in my favour because John
Randall's next line was ages before mine.

He just managed to make it, though. "Right," said he,
the following performance, "tonight . . . *two* biscuits."
That was taking it a bit far, but he said a refusal would
brand me a cissy or whatever (wimps being unknown
at that period) so I took up the challenge.

Out went the lights, into the wings, snatch the biscuits, back onstage. I was in trouble. These weren't
smooth, co-operative biscuits, they were rough and dry
and chunky. From the corner of my eye I checked on
John, whose jaws were working slyly. Was it imagination, or could I see panic in his eyes?

The action of the play rolled on, there were only about
ten lines of dialogue before Randall, poor chump, lost

the game and showed himself up. His cue arrived, and casually, clearly, without the slightest obstruction and not a suspicion of a single, flying crumb, he said his piece. The swine hadn't taken any biscuits, he'd been miming for me.

Richard Briers is a great corpser, I enjoyed trying to make him giggle. We first met in 1957 when I was in Sartre's *Nekrassov* at the Royal Court. Richard's wife Anne was in it, they'd only just been married or were about to be married, so he would come to see her.

Later we were in Tom Stoppard's *The Real Inspector Hound*, playing the two theatre critics who get drawn into the action. Richard and I never got onto the same wavelength as the director, Robert Chetwynd. "We don't want a laugh *there*, do we?" Chetwynd said during a rehearsal. Richard and I just looked at each other; we were in the middle of a comedy scene in a comedy. *Don't want laughs there!* Dear me . . .

So now and then during the play, I'd pull faces at Richard, just to cheer him up. He was at my mercy, the audience had his face in view at that point, but not mine.

I suspect that Robert Chetwynd was in awe of Tom Stoppard, or at least, respected and admired him too much to allow any departure from the script. When I told him I couldn't say a line (and arguing from the viewpoint of writer as well as performer, awkward or literally unspeakable dialogue gets into the best scripts) Chetwynd was alarmed. Tom Stoppard's words mustn't be tampered with.

Of course, when Tom Stoppard arrived to watch a rehearsal and I asked him if there could be a minor alteration to a line giving me problems, he was fine. "Change anything you like, Ronnie."

Lysistrata at the Royal Court caused something of a stir, and a certain amount of corpsing. The director was Greek, Minos Volanakis, and his foible was that scenes he didn't like, he would not rehearse.

It wasn't an easy piece, a lot to learn, difficult music,

seven beats to the bar. There were fourteen scenes and
the day before dress rehearsal, we hadn't linked any
of them. Large cast, obviously one started in different
positions for every scene, and Minos Volanakis stub-
bornly declined to do anything about it. Strange man,
moody, and interested only in . . . well, what interested
him. Which wasn't much help to the rest of us.

The upshot was that James Grout and I and a few
others had our own rehearsal before the formal one. We
brought everyone in and it was, "You go over there and
I'll be over here . . . All right, and then she can move
upstage and . . ." It worked out all right, *Lysistrata* was
a success.

Though not in the eyes of certain people. Aristophanes
imagined women denying sexual favours to their men
in a bid to abolish war. It's a classic play, perfectly
seemly, but in December of 1957 it managed to upset a few activists. There was a disturbance in the
circle, shouting, and leaflets tossed down, claiming,
'THIS PLAY IS DISGUSTING'. (It was nothing of the
kind.)

Not many people were involved but they made a
terrible racket. Jimmy Grout came on, he was one of the
chorus of old men, and announced, in character, "The
gods are angry." This brought fervent applause from the
stalls.

Neil McCarthy, a familiar face on television – you
weren't likely to forget it – played the Athenian herald.
No longer with us, sadly, Neil was a big, tough-looking
man with a tremendous jaw and generally forbidding
aura. He made a terrific heavy and, with that craggy
profile, was everyone's image of a Red Indian brave.
Actually he was a teddy bear, and Neil had a wicked
sense of humour. He always broke me up, because
there'd be this lowering, frowning face and out of it
popped lovely jokes and puns.

Joan Greenwood, another one-of-a-kind performer
with a highly distinctive look and sound, was Lysistrata.

116

Neil listened to her and thought his thoughts, preparing a carefully polished ad-lib to destroy me.

The chorus of old men, me among them, crouched in a group while Lysistrata proclaimed, "Armageddon, it's . . . Armageddon!" as only she could.

And one night, no sooner had she delivered that line, than Neil McCarthy, the swine, whispered in my ear, *"Armageddon outta here!"*

I must sound terribly irresponsible, having admitted that corpsing is unprofessional. But it's also human, often a helpless response to disaster or teasing. I am no more prone to it than most actors, and less so than many. And it isn't just comedy actors who corpse, the most serious and eminent players have succumbed in their time.

Nicol Williamson loved pranks and wasn't above pulling jokes on stage. We were in *A Midsummer Night's Dream*, at the Royal Court again, shared a dressing room and played a lot of poker. Colin Blakely was Bottom, Nicol and I were among the Rude Mechanicals, we had little scrolls which were supposed to be our parts in the Pyramus and Thisbe playlet. On the last night I tucked a poker hand, full house or whatever, behind my scroll and let Nicol see it – then he brought a hand on, beating it.

That was an all-star cast if you like, though it wasn't apparent at the time. Tony Richardson directed, and besides Colin Blakely, there were Robert Lang, Alfred Lynch, Corin Redgrave, Rita Tushingham, Lynn Redgrave, Samantha Eggar . . .

And David Warner.

Nicol Williamson, James Bolam, David and I were all in the same dressing room. It was David's first West End engagement, as I recall, and he'd do the most extraordinary things on stage – wander about, or not move when he was supposed to – believing that was what he *should* do at that point. It was a bit off-putting. We had goes at him: "You really can't suit yourself because the spirit takes you, David. A play is a pre-arranged thing, that's why we have rehearsals." There were frequent arguments about it.

Finally Nicol and I took him on one side. "David, you shouldn't be in this business. It's not going to work for you, you have the wrong temperament, you're just not cut out for it. Maybe if you were a star it might be all right, but . . . Give it up!"

Three years later he was playing Hamlet at Stratford.

Mind you, Nicol could be naughty. The last night, when he was supposed to say, "So farewell, friends, Thus Thisbe ends. Adieu, adieu, adieu," he turned it into, "Cheerio and have a go, Adieu, adieu, adieu."

I've never believed that Shakespeare is sacred, changes can be made, but that seemed a bit much.

Nicol was another great face-puller – it's a common cause of corpsing. You just turn upstage, when they're facing down, and let 'em have it. I'm told that Nigel Patrick's method was even more fiendish: he would know other people's dialogue as well as his own, murmuring it under his breath *while they delivered it*.

Don't run away with the idea that actors are larking about in every performance, or that they do not take things seriously. Most professionals have corpsing anecdotes but after some forty years in the theatre and showbusiness, mine total no more than half a dozen or so. I find it rather charming and reassuring that no matter who the performers or what the type of play, there's an impish spirit behind the façade.

16

RADIO DAZE

I GOT into radio through Knothole Street, Russett Green.

Explaining that cryptic statement, soon after coming to London my agent Peter Eade steered me towards radio. Before the advent of ITV in 1955 it was still *the* mass audience medium. Peter's clients included Joan Sims and Kenneth Williams, both big in radio, so he was well up on that side of things, as in so many others.

He knew that Alastair Scott-Johnston was about to launch a new series with Gert and Daisy. They were Elsie and Doris Waters, sisters of Jack Warner, the *Dixon of Dock Green* actor, and stars in their own right. The Gert and Daisy characters were being moved into a situation comedy, so the scriptwriters – who included Terry Nation, who hadn't yet dreamed up the Daleks for *Dr Who* – had them running a village store at the aforementioned Knothole Street.

Floggit's, the Gert and Daisy show was called, and Alastair Scott-Johnston wanted some new character voices: right up my street, Knothole or otherwise. I got taken on, and so did an ex-child actor, Anthony Newley. He was great fun, a quirky person. 'MONEY ISN'T EVERYTHING – *Old Chinese Proberb*' was printed on his card, he gave them out to everyone. I came in to the studio, so proud of my new suit, and Newley gave me

119

a consoling pat on the shoulder and said, "Never mind, old man, one day you'll have clothes."

Having grown up with radio it was good to be in it, I enjoyed the work and the company. Gert and Daisy were lovely, Newley made me laugh a lot, Hugh Paddick and Joan Sims were in the team. But after two seasons of the series, they didn't want me any more and they didn't want Tony Newley. Alastair Scott-Johnston looked a bit uncomfortable and explained, "Um, basically the two of you are too funny."

It was a compliment we could have done without, but there it was. The feeling being that Tony Newley and I were detracting from Gert and Daisy, restricting their scope, and after all, it was Gert and Daisy's vehicle. In justice to them, I don't believe Elsie and Doris Waters tried to get us dropped, they weren't like that and they'd always been nice to us.

But that wasn't the setback it must have seemed at the time, more BBC work came in, and eventually I appeared in around three hundred programmes.

Next came *Variety Playhouse*, I became a regular on that, and if ever a series earned its title, that was it. You'd have Ted Ray, resident comedian, Harry Worth opening the show and Arthur Askey closing it, with some opera and perhaps Sir Donald Wolfit or Jack Hulbert and Cicely Courtneidge in dramatic excerpts during the programme.

It was educative working with Ted Ray, the cleverest ad-libber of the lot. He'd shield his script and say, "Stop reading my ad-libs." But that was a gag, they were all in his brain and that was like a computer – no hesitation, always an appropriate comeback. The nice thing about Ted was his sense of fun, he couldn't help the wisecracks. Again, Alastair Scott-Johnston was in charge and where many producers can be fussy, give the performers an endless stream of notes, that wasn't Alastair's style. He let you get on with it, trusted your judgment, and rarely intervened.

Then came a rehearsal of a sketch in which Ted and I were in an office, and Patricia Hayes was the secretary. Alastair hadn't given Ted a note in months, but this time he suggested a minor change of emphasis – "Why not make it a throwaway remark instead of angry?"

Instantly, Ted threw down his script in mock exasperation, screwed up his face and groaned, "Alastair, why are you always interfering?"

Delightful person, consummate professional yet didn't make heavy weather of it. I missed Ted when he went on to other things. Vic Oliver conducted the *Variety Playhouse* orchestra and did sketches as well for a while, and then Alastair told me he was bringing in "a new young lad, I think you'll work well together."

And the lad was Leslie Crowther and we were chums from the minute we met. I wish he'd do more comedy. Leslie does cabaret and after-dinner speeches but a generation must be growing up who associate him with *The Price Is Right* and don't realise how funny he can be. A well educated, sensitive man, too. I remember sitting and listening to a beautiful aria being rehearsed for that week's programme, and glancing around to find Leslie in tears. He'd been working very hard for a couple of weeks and the music and song released the emotion and it was pouring out of him.

Every week a stage personality did a monologue or took part in a scene from a famous play. All the top performers took part, it was one of the highspots for me. Fay Compton came along and, despite being in her sixties at the time, looked beautiful. She was wearing a blue crinoline, an early nineteenth-century costume, I have an idea she was reading from Jane Austen.

Yes, this was sound-only, but the programmes were recorded before an audience. You were expected to dress up a bit, though she would have, anyway. Miss Compton completed her piece, the show went on, but performers had to stay until the end in case anything had to be re-recorded, minor fluffs corrected.

121

Alastair Scott-Johnston did come through on the speaker when the programme finished, asking for Miss Compton to re-record just a couple of sentences. The audience waited patiently but she was nowhere to be found – people raced around the building and located her in the canteen.

Silence was called for, the audience perked up, and onto the stage came not the crinoline lady but Fay Compton in backstage dress: slacks, beret, a big sling bag over her shoulder. There was a strong aura of "Any more fares please." Leslie and I couldn't help chuckling at the transformation from Jane Austen to bus conductress. Fay Compton's eyes were twinkling, she could see the funny side.

June Whitfield was another *Variety Playhouse* regular and she, Leslie and I enjoyed working as a trio. In 1963, on what was still the Home Service, *Crowther's Crowd* gave us our own series. Maybe I can make a pop millionaire wince by exhuming the *Radio Times* comment on our backing group: "Mickie Most and The Minute Men lace the programme with coffee bar rhythms." Mickie outlasted the coffee bars.

The year *The Two Ronnies* began, 1971, I had my own series, *Lines From My Grandfather's Forehead*, allowing me to write and sing pastiche folk and music hall songs, among other things, so that was enjoyable. Of course, *the* radio show was *The Navy Lark*. It ran for years, twenty weeks at a time, and people loved it. (When the BBC tried updating it by bringing the characters ashore for *The TV Lark*, there was such outrage among addicts that it had to be switched back again in a hurry.)

"*The rotten ol' rottens . . .*" may strike a chord. I was Able Seaman Johnson, grumbling away. And that hopeless engine-room officer, Lieutenant Queeg, who didn't know the names of any of the machinery, and spoke in that very precise, educated Scottish manner . . . borrowed from Chick Murray.

Working on *The Navy Lark* was a romp. Listeners

revelled in it but we had just as much fun aboard HMS *Troutbridge*, sailing along there in Broadcasting House. With Leslie Phillips, Jon Pertwee and Michael Bates – he was a character, a real wag – around, things were never too solemn. There'd always be a leg-pull or wind-up in the air, our producer as target. Deliberate mistakes were a regular ploy, varied by sudden attacks of denseness when, immensely helpful, we still couldn't *quite* understand what he wanted.

Leaving after nine happy years was a wrench, and not the easiest of decisions. I'd be going down the gangplank from the most popular venture of its kind, and the security guaranteed by that. The trouble was that *The Frost Report*, David Frost's new BBC series, went out live and *The Navy Lark* was recorded on a Sunday. It had to be, with the cast so often committed to stage plays.

My friends on HMS *Troutbridge* teased me unmercifully when I left. They said it was the first known instance of a rat deserting an unsinkable ship!

17

WATCH YOUR CONTINUITY

IF there's no fish at the end of your line then you can't land the damn thing, agreed?

That bit of dazzling wisdom and insight got me a lot of stick a few years ago, but I stand by it. Radical members of Equity, my union, were making a huge fuss over 'Right to work', threatening to barricade themselves inside theatres and goodness knows what else, in defence of their right to be employed.

I wrote an open letter saying nobody in the business had that right. And if they did, acting would fill up with people who were no good. Rights don't come into it, the decisive thing is luck.

Naturally there was a deluge of replies to me, quite an uproar, with accusations of selfishness and arrogance – "Just because you think you're talented" – when that was a word I hadn't mentioned. I maintain that ours is an absolutely precarious trade. If you don't get a single job, it is not your fault, necessarily.

Believing that is not arrogance but the reverse. Certainly one must be willing to work, and have an optimum amount of ability. People all over the place have as much as I did, without making it. There were some fine actors in repertory companies with me, but they just got squeezed out, never had a proper chance.

Luck: I got into the West End through Peter Hall. We happened to get on, my face fitted. But I met him because

124

I'd wanted to be at home for a while, and wallow in the luxury of learning only one play a fortnight.

Luck: in the 'fifties, Jimmy Gilbert, then a radio and stage producer, was preparing a revue with Stanley Baxter, *On The Brighter Side*, and came along to *Variety Playhouse* to check me out. Stanley Baxter and Betty Marsden were the stars, and we played in London and took the show on tour, Oxford, Edinburgh, Glasgow. *On The Brighter Side* was full of pretty, gifted girls – such as Amanda Barrie, Una Stubbs and Judy Carne but apart from David Kernan, who did a lot of the songs, I was one of the few chaps involved.

That meant that when Stanley lost his voice, I had to fill in for him. I had to follow myself – do a sketch, go off, and come on again immediately, which was strenuous. But Jimmy Gilbert must have remembered my work, because when he produced a BBC television series with Jimmy Edwards, *The Seven Faces of Jim*, he gave me "a couple of little bits" in it. And they were little, neither here nor there really, though most welcome at this stage in my career.

Terence Alexander had something better, in the third episode. He was playing villain to Jimmy's dupe, as a con-man. Something happened, either there was a mix-up and Terence Alexander found that he'd been booked for a film as well, or he fell ill. The upshot was that he did the read-through and that was the last we saw of him.

Frank Muir, who was writing the show, with Denis Norden of course, said, "I think Ronnie could take over, he's only doing a couple of lines, we can lose them or cover them somehow." I agreed to have a go – they couldn't have stopped me! – and since this con-man character, Sid Figgins, poses as very grand but in reality is a nobody, a real guttersnipe, I suggested that I play him as Welsh.

"Sid Figgins wouldn't be able to sound grand and carry it off, if he was English," I reasoned, "but if he's

125

Welsh the class barrier disappears, most Englishmen wouldn't be able to tell." So that's what I did, it went well, everybody was delighted.

The following week, expecting my couple of lines, I was told that I'd be doing a two-hander with Jimmy Edwards, a lovely part as a lighthouse keeper. Suddenly, after a couple of screenings, I was being featured in a peak time series with a household-name star.

Sorry to harp on the point, but if Terence Alexander hadn't dropped out, I might well have drifted through that series, not been in the next, and then . . . who knows? It wasn't my talent that put him out – *it was luck*. I suppose I've made the most of it, been an opportunist if you like. You spot the opportunity, think *This could be good, don't mess this up, get it right*, you work extra hard and the adrenalin spurts. As an American golf champion said, it was strange how his luck improved the more he practised! Granted, one took advantage of luck. But it had to be there before one could.

We finished up doing a score of those Jimmy Edwards shows, *Seven Faces of Jim*, *Six More Faces*, *Yet More Faces*. Jimmy was lovely to work with, he didn't suffer fools gladly, wanted to get on and do it, but then so did I. June Whitfield and I were regulars, they revived *The Glums* from the radio hit, *Take It From Here*, and I was Ron to her Eth, with Jimmy, of course, as Pa Glum.

It stood me in good stead with the BBC, for when it finished, Frank Muir teamed me with Leslie Phillips, my old shipmate, for *Foreign Affairs*. That series was about diplomats, Leslie the Foreign Office twit and me the Russian Embassy twit. Russian was outside the voice-repertoire I'd built up, so it needed a bit of study.

Names and wordplay have always tickled me, perhaps it's a trait inherited from my father. (Doing *The Real Inspector Hound*, I was bold enough to remind Tom Stoppard that the dialogue involved people called McCoy and McKay, which was confusing. "Give me another name, then," said Tom. Driving home that evening, I noticed Puckeridge on a Hertfordshire signpost, and proposed it next morning – I could just imagine Richard Briers saying 'Puckeridge'. So one edition of *Inspector Hound* has McCoy and another that name off a signpost.)

Anyway, while playing that Soviet diplomat, I was approached by an opera singer turned film producer called Sam Gallu, splendid name. He was making an espionage thriller about a CIA agent under pressure in London, and was looking for somebody to play the hero's shady Greek acquaintance. That seemed marvellous, since the star was Van Heflin, a real Hollywood figure.

I read a scene for Sam, using my Russian accent, and he complimented me on my marvellous Greek accent! "Can you grow a moustache?" Sam asked, and I promised to try. The film was *The Man Outside*, though for obvious reasons we nicknamed it *The Shooting of Sam Gallu*. It did all right, got some good reviews, and still surfaces on television. After it came out there were some letters asking how I'd perfected the Greek accent for this Vetaxas character . . . when I'd gone through it under the impression it was a Russian one. Apparently they're quite similar; certainly when I do them!

Van Heflin was a seasoned Hollywood veteran, friendly and helpful. I got to know him a little bit because the film's set-up, the situation and atmosphere, emerges in a long conversation between the CIA man and his Greek contact, at the outset.

"Watch your continuity," was Van's opening remark when we started work. That baffled me, so he explained, "Don't ever eat, don't ever drink, don't ever smoke. You can have a beer or a cigarette, just don't use them."

That way, when the director and editor came to cut the footage, they could cut anywhere. Otherwise a glass of beer one moment on the table, the next at your lips could make the close-ups unusable and you would always be seen in long-shot. Valuable advice which has stood me in good stead in all subsequent filming.

127

The Man Outside's early sequences were being shot on location around Kensington at night. Usually night filming means a three p.m. start with everyone knocking off at one in the morning, but for this we started at eight and went on until dawn – in theory.

In practice, come two in the morning, Sam Gallu took Van Heflin into his caravan, there were several on the set, and they'd kill a bottle together. After an hour and a half, Sam would emerge, saying, "Let's go home, the old man's drunk."

Maybe Van Heflin got tired after the first four-hour stint of the night or possibly Sam Gallu didn't like filming then, but either way, work was knocked on the head. It was still hard work for me, but fascinating, finding out about a completely different sphere.

More and more, though, I was working in television. I did some plays, a spot in *The Avengers*, an episode of *The Saint* – Roger Moore was marvellous, wisecracking and clowning around up to the very moment the clapper-board was snapped. And briefly, I did something very odd for the top current affairs magazine of the time, BBC's *Tonight*. This was television's first living strip-cartoon, written by Bernard Levin, an unlikely strip-cartoonist. The idea was to make joky, mildly satirical comments on subjects not quite strong enough for a full interview. Prunella Scales was Awful Evelyn, I was her Uncle Leslie, and we appeared with our heads stuck through a cartoon backdrop, rather like those Edwardian seaside-photograph things. Evelyn was a schoolgirl asking innocently shrewd questions; it didn't work, and with almost indecent haste she was shot with a cardboard bullet and thus ended B. Levin's career in TV Light Entertainment. I wonder if he ever found another line of work?

But the fiasco did introduce me to Ned Sherrin, who'd launched *That Was The Week That Was* and talked of a new young presenter he had found, David Frost, whom Ned believed might be quite good. Ned Sherrin seemed to be mulling things over, whether to keep David on every show or alternate him with somebody else. I'd seen Frost in the first programme and told Ned I thought he was excellent. Ned nodded and said, "Yes, I think he'll be doing it."

I doubt whether I had anything to do with deciding that, since *TW3* was a runaway success and David Frost's personality came right out of the screen, in a sense he *was* *TW3*, despite the vast stable of writers and performers involved. Anyway, if I *did* add a grain of support in those early days, bread cast upon the waters came back buttered.

This is a glimpse of the obvious, but David is extremely astute. Some very recent undergraduates catapulted to his level of instant fame would have thanked their stars, kept delivering the mixture as before, and risked paying the price when the vogue for them was over. David was playing the long game, however, already thinking ahead.

Realising that an *enfant terrible*'s life, by definition, must be short, he set about diversifying a bit. His next series, *The Frost Report*, would play down his previous image of barbed, spiteful wit. In any case, he loved one-liners and they didn't need to be satirical.

For me, *The Frost Report* came out of the blue. When it was being planned, two people – David, and Jimmy Gilbert – suggested recruits for the team. Jimmy put me forward, David suggested Ronnie Corbett, whom he'd seen at Danny La Rue's nightclub, and John Cleese, whom he'd got to know through university.

Neither Ronnie knew it, but a partnership was about to be formed.

18

TOWN AND GOWN

IMAGINE Monty Python joining forces with *At Last The 1948 Show*, an outstanding series of its day, and The Goodies, and you'll understand the promise behind David Frost's entry into light entertainment.

John Cleese, Graham Chapman, Terry Jones, Michael Palin, Tim Brooke-Taylor, Bill Oddie and Marty Feldman were just some of the writers. All had won their spurs and had glowing reputations, I didn't know them well or even at all, in some cases. It was slightly daunting, that first day.

But it was heartening to spot Ronnie Corbett arriving for the initial gathering, a familiar face and an acquaintance from the Buckstone Club. Naturally we tended to cling together.

The others were very 'varsity, or so it seemed to us. They didn't mean to be, they were most friendly, but they couldn't help it. John Cleese was very grand, even then – physically, I mean, looking down at the world literally from on high. Up there in the clouds, a bit withdrawn and abstracted, with that great Desperate Dan chin – I'd love to see him playing Desperate Dan!

Coming from Oxford, I saw it in terms of Town and Gown, no hostility, not a trace of it, but two camps. (Ronnie Corbett and Ronnie Barker were a little camp on their own? Needs rephrasing.) But you get the idea. Ronnie C. and I came from different backgrounds, mine

130

was theatre and he had cut his teeth as a stand-up comic, but I liked comedy and he liked acting and the pair of us were grammar school boys. Inevitably we were readier to bounce ideas off each other and compare notes.

Everybody worked with everybody else, of course. I'd do a sketch with John Cleese, Ronnie C. appeared with others in the team as often as me. But somehow they started writing occasional sketches for the two of us. By the second season of the series it was happening often. And then the programme won the premier international TV award, the Golden Rose of Montreux, with *Frost Over England* in 1967. Apart from the thrill, it did all of us a lot of good, professionally.

There were headlines, interviews with all concerned, and job offers. By the same token, while it's lovely to win awards, one shouldn't get too inflated a self-image out of them. Once I came back to England with one, a delighted BBC held a reception to celebrate my prowess, and Tom Sloan, Head of Light Entertainment, made much of me. It was a real arm-round-the-shoulder job. "Now tell me, Ronnie, isn't there something we can do for you . . . ?"

"Actually, there is." (Well, he had asked.) "Er, would it be possible to have a parking space in the TV Centre park at White City, please? Not a permanent one, just when I'm working there."

Poor Tom's face fell, he started edging away, muttering, "Oh, that's nothing to do with me, I can't promise that." So I went on sneaking in with the car!

Funny place, Television Centre. It came to be a home of sorts, *The Two Ronnies* base, but the Beeb didn't always see it that way. I applied to join the BBC club, it's on an upper floor, not a spectacular place but nice for meeting family and friends without leaving the building. All the staff belong, it's very democratic . . . but they turned me down.

Ever afterwards, I not only gatecrashed but took sly pleasure in signing people in, including some who worked for the BBC full-time. Everybody assumed that

I must be a member. "That's all right, I'll sign you in," I'd say, and everybody was happy!

The Frost Report ended when David diversified even more, set up a consortium when fresh ITV franchises were awarded in the 'sixties, and helped to launch London Weekend Television. Just to keep his hand in, he anchored three shows a week on the new station, right through the weekend. Each night had a different tone, from hard-hitting to escapist.

"I want all of you to come with me," said David, and most of us did. John Cleese decided that he wanted to stop performing for a while and stick to writing instead. It had been worrying him, he'd look white around the gills before starting a sketch. It wouldn't have surprised me if he had stopped entirely when *The Frost Report* finished, because clearly he was not enjoying it all that much any more. Thank goodness he didn't quit, else we would have lost the Ministry of Silly Walks, lovely *Fawlty Towers*, and so much else to treasure.

I've never put much stock in the idea that shows or people lose something by switching from BBC to ITV or vice-versa. Some people felt Morecambe and Wise weren't as good when they changed, and for my money, that was nonsense, they were good as ever, and that was the best.

But *Frost on Sunday* was a bit different, we went up a gear, simply because it went out live and was that much more hectic. Josephine Tewson joined the team and became a friend, she partnered me in the Lord Rustless shows and my final series, *Clarence*. Ronnie C. and I were used to thinking on our feet and dashing around, which was just as well. In two years we did nearly fifty of those shows, up to twenty-six weeks at a stretch, involving lord knows how many sketches.

It was a bit like my radio stint in *Variety Playhouse*, for David got endless celebrity guests and we met them in the hospitality room at Wembley Studios afterwards – Peter Sellers, Tom Jones, Sammy Davis. I was busy with my autograph album. (Joy says that I'd be hopeless as a proper, big-deal star because I am hopelessly star-struck! Doesn't matter, I collect everything, including autographs. Among them is John Gielgud's, on the back of a chit from Oxford Playhouse gaining me free entry to a local cinema. I went up to London with some friends, waited by the stage door, and although getting a reproachful murmur of, "Rather late for autographs, isn't it?" added Sir John's to my hoard.)

The live, last-moment element in *Frost on Sunday* sparked a running gag which viewers never saw. The joke was on us, anyway. It concerned a quickie sketch at the end, when we had to smear our faces with black camouflage streaks and be seen in commando uniform, creeping through bushes. Then we all had to stand up and start crooning, 'She's My Lady Love', minstrel-fashion.

It was frenetic, especially for a fifteen-second sketch – sprinting to the dressing room, on with the uniform, black up, dash back to our start-line in those studio bushes. No sooner had we got there than the floor manager hissed, "It's all off, chaps, the show's over-running." Rather let down, we trooped away.

The same thing happened the next week. By the third week we were disgruntled, and the fourth week David's little army mutinied. This time we hurried away but didn't get ready. When they said, "Right, you're on, we're ready," we told them that they might be – but we weren't! David just put in another joke off the clipboard and we had made our point.

Ronnie C. and I were working for David's firm now, David Paradine Productions, which arranged for each of us to have solo series on ITV while his programme was off the air. Ronnie got *No That's Me Over Here*, situation comedy, and mine was *The Ronnie Barker Playhouse*. I loved that (although I hated the title), for it gave me the opportunity to create a different character every week in a string of half-hour playlets. More than one, come to that, when I was a failed escapologist, busking in the street, and a Lord Rustless type of old buffer watching him.

On the surface things were going swimmingly, each Ronnie in a show of his own, plus *Frost on Sunday*. Nothing could stop us, or could it? Yes, it could.

I was about to get the sack.

Nothing to do with me, not directly. The person doing the firing was friendly, even admiring, she liked my work and wanted to use me. *But* . . .

Stella Richman started her career as an actress, got married, began again as script editor for television, and learning the business from the inside, became Britain's first top woman executive. She was recruited as programme controller at London Weekend. Stella was, and indeed is, a charming, attractive, super-intelligent person; at the same time, she knew her own mind and was determined to be the boss. Fair enough, that was what they paid her for.

Calling me in for a confidential meeting, Stella Richman explained that she couldn't do with Paradine Productions, could not live with them. Or in her more elegant phrasing, "I am just not compatible with the administration at Paradine."

While I digested that – why was she confiding in me? – Stella went on, "I've told David Frost that as long as this situation continues with Paradine, I cannot employ him. Or employ you either." Perhaps the implication was that if I broke with Paradine Productions then I could sign another contract for programmes with LWT. But that wasn't on; Paradine hadn't done us any harm, exactly the opposite. Ronnie Corbett felt the same way.

We were out.

And that was the genesis of *The Two Ronnies*. It came about through getting the sack.

The British Academy of Film and Television Arts annual awards ceremony was being held at the London Palladium that year, and the *Frost on Sunday* team of David, Ronnie C., Jo Tewson and I was asked to provide some entertainment as part of the evening.

That was fine, everyone wants to do the Palladium – I never dreamed that my variety debut would be made there, when we did the stage version of *The Two Ronnies* – and someone wrote us a sketch.

I played Henry VIII and Ronnie was Cardinal Wolsey; a very camp, Jewish Wolsey, with a big cigar and a costume with a twenty-yard train, he was hilarious. It was a singing-dancing number, Jo Tewson playing all six wives, amazing when you think about it. The audience loved it, and this wasn't your standard audience, all the television overlords were there.

Bill Cotton and Paul Fox of the BBC were sitting together. During our sketch, Bill whispered to Paul Fox, "What about a series with those two?" Of course, Stella Richman's bombshell wasn't public knowledge, as far as anyone knew we were ITV performers. "It's going to cost us," said Bill Cotton, "but we might pull it off. What about it?"

Paul told him to have a go.

So Bill set up a meeting and asked, "Would you come and do a series for us? Just the two of you, not David Frost. Come over to the BBC, can't we entice you?"

Ronnie and I looked at each other. Poker-faced, I said, "I think we might be enticed." Ronnie nodded solemnly. "Yes, Bill," we said, "yes, we can be enticed."

He didn't get the joke. I don't believe that Bill Cotton ever did find out that we'd been sacked when he made that approach. This is an odd business: often when you're not wanted over *there*, you're less of a hot property over *here*. He might have gone sour on us.

As things turned out, he'd have kicked himself.

Deal done, a name had to be found for the new show. Hard to believe, but we couldn't think of one at first. Then somebody remembered a familiar remark at rehearsals for the various Frost programmes . . . "The two Ronnies can do that sketch." We had our title, all that remained was to create something which would run for a dozen series and the next seventeen years.

19

BLACK MY DOOBERRIES

BILL COTTON had snatched us away from ITV, as he thought. Now what could we give the BBC?

The first *Two Ronnies* went out in April 1971 and, having seen tapes of it, I'm honestly surprised that it did so well. Everybody felt it was going to be a great show – our wives were in the audience and they said the atmosphere was electric – but that launching edition did not show a high degree of confidence. (Joy chuckles and nudges me when that tape is run, pointing out that Ronnie C. and I keep gulping nervously. Condemned men!)

The format was bred out of *Frost On Sunday*, it wasn't particularly original. David did one-liners to camera and we liked that, but rapport hadn't been established between us and the studio audience – and through them, people watching at home – so we decided to do that routine as characters, the newsreaders.

We really tried to act the parts, and quickie sketches were inserted – 'Ronnie Corbett reports' – but it looks strange now. That changed because we were doing sketches elsewhere in the programme. The style evolved, the newsreaders faded down and the Two Ronnies made the jokes.

It was the era of classic serials, so I wrote one for us, 'Hampton Wick'. That introduced Maddie Smith who (slipping into something more comfortable, with one

136

of my *Two Ronnies* personas) brought these enormous attributes to the show. She didn't know where they came from, said Maddie, they just appeared overnight. We didn't believe a word of it!

No, Maddie was this sweet, delicate, innocent little girl . . . with an opulent, very emphatic bosom. She popped out once or twice, in the studio and on location filming. Ronnie C. was chasing her round a building, and when Maddie emerged the other side, the camera crew went, "Oh my goodness" and had to cut. A few seconds later, after a pause for thought.

She was The Pretty Girl while Ronnie C. and I played all the other parts, which was hard work. For the Victorian episode we did a sort of Oliver Twist story with me as Bill Sikes. It looked convincing because I was suffering from terrible 'flu at the time! We were being all these different people, masters of disguise, and Maddie was always exactly the same girl but nobody noticed, or if they did, they didn't mind.

The pastiche classic serial led on to parodies of most TV dramas of the day, from *Colditz* and *The Regiment* to *Star Trek* and *Upstairs Downstairs*.

I wrote seventy-five per cent of the shows at first, but not the imaginary news items and the one-liners like, "What d'you get if you cross a very tall chamber pot with a table tennis ball? A ping-pong piddle-high po." They were a specialised art and a lot of writers contributed.

People still remind me of personal favourites. "A cement mixer has collided with a prison van. Motorists are asked to be on the look-out for sixteen hardened criminals." Or the Irish Domesday Book, denounced as a forgery after study by typewriting experts.

Inconsequential, larky, apparently casual – and we read two hundred a week to select twenty, of which a dozen might make it as far as the screen. Outrageous puns were a feature but we tried to resist the real groaners, the excruciating stuff.

I loved doing Spoonerisms but they were swine to master. Named after an eminent Victorian, Dr Spooner, whose tongue-tangles made him come out with extra-ordinary sayings, they are created by swopping consonants at the beginning of words, and sometimes the middles of words into the bargain.

We did an entire four-minute Spoonerisms sketch once, quite an achievement. The trouble is, one thinks, "Right, Spoonerism coming up," but the subconscious automatically puts things right – Spoonerising the Spoonerism! Instead of announcing that you're going to "Tump into a jaxi", it comes out "Jump into a taxi," which leaves an audience waiting for the joke . . . When it flows, though, it's glorious: in a gardening sketch, for instance, "I'm going to rip out and pick a few noses, and spray my flies for greenbeans. I'll probably black my dooberries as well." Lovely.

Providing you didn't do it too often at the same point, the studio audience loved fluffs. It let them see how a show is put together, made them insiders. Sometimes I've deliberately got it wrong again after a genuine mistake, just to enjoy the pleasure it created.

Part of the magic of *The Two Ronnies* was the atmosphere, somehow it percolated into TV sets at home. We did everything to keep the studio audience warm – you'd pull silly faces, shove your glasses up your nose, *anything*, right up to the opening word of the next sketch. When there was a filmed item, we didn't let the studio crew change scenery or adjust equipment, which can happen. We valued the audience's concentration too much for that.

Ronnie Corbett was a peerless mood-setter, of course. *The Two Ronnies* never used a warm-up man – there are professionals who do very little else, they're specialists on call for various series – but Ronnie C. always did it for us.

It's a shame that people at home couldn't share that fun. Joy and I have heard some of his warm-up routine for the best part of twenty years and *still* we crack up at certain lines. He's got this great stuff about his deprived childhood: "We were so poor that when I broke my glasses we had to have them boarded up . . . I couldn't afford clothes until I was fourteen, then my mother bought me a hat – so I could look out of the window!"

That's why his cabaret act is superb, he has at least six hours of prime material and from that he selects not even the cream but the real gold, the nuggets.

Reverting to those fluffs for a moment, people can't laugh twice at the same joke, let alone three times. Bringing us to all that terrible canned laughter which we were accused of putting into the show. So-called canned laughter, actually, and it wasn't cheating to use it.

To be mildly technical, all live audience show's laughter is controlled. There have to be special microphones to catch audience reaction, the pots as they are called. Leave the pots open all the time, and the performers' voices sound hollow, the quality is poor. So up in the control room, knobs are twisted when a punchline's delivered, the pots open to catch the laugh, then close again for the next line of dialogue. Canned laughter? I don't think so.

But when one of us fluffed a line, then repeated it on a re-take, the original laughter might be used. Not wrong, in my submission – the audience understood the gag, it was just slightly mangled. They'd laugh when one did it all over again, perfectly, but it would be polite laughter, not the real thing.

Now in America, they *do* use canned laughter. Ronnie C. and I broke our journey to Australia in Los Angeles, stopping long enough to take part in something called *The Big Show*, hosted by Victor Borge. Loretta Swit, Hotlips of *M.A.S.H.* was on the bill and I prostrated myself and kissed her feet, much to the audience's approval. The audience . . . what there was of it!

You see, the programme started letting people in at seven in the evening, and more than an hour later all

139

they'd seen was a man wandering onstage to tune the piano. It worried the life out of me, didn't seem right, discourteous at best.

"That's all right," said the producer, "they don't have to sit, they can go out and have a meal or something."

We went on to do our piece just after midnight, and the place was virtually deserted by then, far more empty seats than occupied ones.

"Great, that was great," the producer enthused. Ronnie and I were depressed, there'd been hardly any laughs.

"Oh, the laughs will be there," the producer promised. And he was right, they had this machine like a synthesiser, for playing laughter and applause rather than music.

The chap playing it was a virtuoso – you played this thing like a piano. He gave me the bizarre information that the laughter tracks were so old, half the people on it must be dead. Hysterical laughter from beyond the grave . . . frightening!

Keeping genuine laughter flowing was a tremendous challenge. The key ingredient was material, we struggled to get it and, when we had it, to improve the scripts. That might not sound unusual, but it was. One famous comedian, lovable man, used to turn up on Tuesdays to start work on his series and ask, "What are we doing on Sunday, then?" The scripts would be slapped down in front of him and he'd bring as much comedy and fun to it as he could manage. It never occurred to him to query and reject and demand better material.

I do have a reputation for being awkward. (A friend suggested that other people might be the awkward ones; while not necessarily the case, it would help me stop worrying about it!) Perfectionist or just pernickety, a fusspot, I was all for doing it again, to get something exactly right.

The Two Ronnies was seen by up to nineteen million people, one can't imagine that many. The only way I could grasp it was to picture a football crowd, say one hundred thousand for a Cup Final, then ten such crowds to make the million, then one hundred and ninety arenas, jam-packed, up in the sky.

Sometimes during a sketch I'd get that mental picture and if I had slurred a word or muffed a move, even fractionally, I would wonder: "Do I want all those people to see that?" The answer was always the same. "Let's do it again, please."

And I'd follow everything through, especially when it was something I had written, from pen on paper to filming, working with the director. A lot can be done at the editing stage and that side had fascinated me ever since Van Heflin and "Watch your continuity." It's drudgery; very slow, fiddly, repetitive work as you create an atmosphere or smooth out the transition from exterior filming to a studio shot, make sure the sound is right, lose the shadow of a microphone boom. All sorts of details – viewers are more sophisticated today but they just watch the programme, they aren't consciously aware of visual techniques and whether it was a close-up or a long shot and so forth. What they *are* aware of, consciously or otherwise, is the feel of a show, whether it's smooth.

And that overall impression doesn't happen by itself, it has to be created. Arguably I made a nuisance of myself. It caused extra work and pressure for me – and others – but I was aiming for longevity. We could have taken easier options, worried less . . . but I doubt whether *The Two Ronnies* would have lasted more than six seasons.

Longevity raises the point that Ronnie C. and I kept making, patiently and politely, for year after year. We weren't a double act, just two friends and solo performers who happened to do one series in partnership.

Professionally speaking it was a marriage; no, better than that, a marriage without ups and downs. The happiest marriages have those, even if it's no more than a minor disagreement over the best place to hang a picture. Ronnie C. and I never differed as seriously as that!

Reporters found it hard to believe, but it wasn't a front. Then again, apart from physical build, we are very similar as people. We have strong, supportive wives – both taller than us! – we aren't nightclubbers and hellraisers, we love our families and value family life. Ronnie C. is mad about golf and I don't play, but he knows better than to talk golf at me, so that's all right.

The main factor in *The Two Ronnies*' success, I'm sure, is that we are on the same comedy wavelength. We read sketches in isolation, marking them with up to three ticks or a cross for a no-no. Comparing scripts at rehearsal, ninety-five per cent of ticks and crosses would be identical, one of us might as well have marked both. Our policy was that if one of us was dubious about a sketch during rehearsal and said so, out it went, even if the other partner quite liked it. The nearest thing to a savage row, ever, came down to Ronnie C. saying he couldn't do something, me replying that we'd have to think of a way, and one being found. It might just as well be the other way around, with me jibbing and Ronnie C. encouraging.

After so long together, it was extraordinary that we never had a fight nor a falling out, never a disagreement of any consequence. But there it is. Maybe our strength lay in the things we were not: not a double act, and not comic and feed. As two actors regularly appearing together, we struck a balance. If I had most of the funny lines in one sketch, Ronnie got plenty in the next. That brought constant variety, a changing ratio, within the format of what became a bit of an institution. Balance was important, and we dug our toes in to achieve it. Bill Cotton wanted shows to go out soon after they were made, and the one time he over-ruled us it was chaos.

As I've said, Ronnie C. and I always agreed on material we thought was good, only borderline cases might leave one of us uncertain. But we weren't infallible, and sometimes the audience didn't agree. It wasn't a problem, because normally we would have recorded four sketches and have time for only three – there'd be a proven reserve ready to replace the failure.

On this single occasion the show was being transmitted shortly after the recording and we had to scrabble around trying to get it right. We went to Bill and said, "Look, you can't do it this way . . . we can't, anyway." And he gave in, reversing his decision.

Basically, although we recorded different editions weekly and of course the mini-series had to be shown in sequence, *The Two Ronnies* was a mountain of material which could be sorted into the eventual series.

In the early days we made eight shows to a season, then six a year. Eight feels *four* longer than six!

The Two Ronnies occupied about half the year, even if some fans felt the shows ended too quickly and the seasons should have been longer as well. By the end, filming alone took up six weeks.

We stopped doing parody serials, we'd done so many, and the films came in, all sorts of styles and genres, including a Viking epic – Ronnie C. was made to be a ravening Norseman! And the films also replaced the original finale of the show, those musical numbers. We had loved them but, again, we'd explored every possibility.

After six weeks filming and a fortnight's editing came another six weeks, one per edition, in the studio. That's three months or more, but the writing had to be done first, material needed to be ready long in advance so that scenery-makers, wardrobe people and other technicians could get started.

The sheer scale of preparation was enormous. A side-effect being that gradually, on the writing side, my ideas started drying up. Anyone can start a comedy sketch but it takes a good man to finish it. A two-minute sketch just as much as a half-hour comedy needs an idea, so you get through a lot of them.

I'd have been grateful for ideas, we were always on the lookout for material, yet in twelve seasons, hardly half a dozen unsolicited, amateur sketches were usable. Hundreds came in, naturally.

And then I got this wonderful letter, a fan letter really, with the seeds of just about the most popular sketch ever presented in *The Two Ronnies*.

20

BILLHOOKS, KNOCKERS AND MRS WHITEHOUSE

A COUPLE who ran a hardware shop at Hayes, not far from our home at Pinner, wrote in saying they enjoyed the show, and mentioned funny things which cropped up in their business. There'd been a lovely cross-purposes when the chap presented a customer with four candles – which he'd just heard him ask for – but what had actually been ordered was fork handles. Somebody else asked if they stocked garden hoes, and that turned out to be hose, as in watering.

People can speak standard English, perfectly clearly, and still be misunderstood. It was such a good idea that I sat down and started evolving a sketch about it. One needed a dozen or so sound-alikes; it took a bit of thinking out but was great fun and more often than not, when anyone talks to me about *The Two Ronnies*, the fork-handles sketch is remembered.

We did it on television and then for the Palladium season. As I've mentioned, Ronnie had variety experience but my first appearance in variety was topping the bill at the London Palladium. That must be unique. Even though a lot of the material had been done before in the studio, it was terrifying – and uplifting.

Any audience gets the adrenalin flowing. Ronnie C. and I used to psych each other up during filming for *The Two Ronnies*; you had to be about twenty per cent higher to make up for having no audience. "Energy, energy, energy," we'd tell each other, just before each take.

No need for that at the London Palladium! The adrenalin was certainly going then. The public expected some of those complicated singing numbers, and there was no autocue. I had this 'Phil The Fluter's Ball' parody, 'Phyllis Hooter's Ball', as a Chelsea pensioner remembering a society dance he'd attended. The lyric was virtually all names, "*There was Jean, there was June, there was Janet, there was Jennifer and Jane and Joyce and Jacqueline and Juliet and Joan. There was Milly who was silly, there was Sally who was pally, there was Annie with her grannie and Fanny on her own.*"

Joy sent me a telegram, "ALL MY LOVE, AS ALWAYS – GET IT RIGHT!" I'd been singing the blessed thing for weeks, at home, even in my sleep!

Imagining a television audience in those stadiums in the sky was one thing but hearing two thousand people laughing in the Palladium was marvellous. Though large, it's an intimate theatre and the people seem very close, stacked up, a living wall, and when the wall is laughing . . . terrific!

Just as had happened with Glénn Melvyn at Bramhall, Ronnie C. and I could discover what worked best, and build on that, night by night. The fork-handles sketch was embellished during the run, but for a long time the tag, the finish, made me unhappy.

Ronnie C. was the shopkeeper and I was this terrible gump, an idiot in a woolly hat, asking for items sounding eyebrow-raising yet which turned out to be innocent. The original tag was that Ronnie snatched the shopping list from me, snapped, "That's it, I'm not serving you any more." His assistant took over and quite unruffled, asked, "What sort of billhooks do you want?"

That displeased me, I hated the implication of the word. Then I thought of bringing in Rikki Howard, a very spectacular girl, as the assistant. "Yes sir," she'd say, displaying the cleavage, "what sort of knockers were you looking for?'' Still a double entendre, but a lighter feel to it somehow, comic-postcard spirit.

That may strike you as surprisingly prim and prissy and more than a bit hypocritical. "Come off it," I've been told, "*The Two Ronnies* could be rude, near the knuckle and all that." But we always made sure that the audience had an escape route; children or a maiden aunt could hear something with a double meaning but at least there *was* an alternative meaning, silly enough to be amusing. "Freeze the brass buttons off a flunkey," that sort of thing.

Easy for me to pontificate, is the other retort, because *The Two Ronnies* were middle-of-the-road comedians. But we tried to be all over the road, cover a wide swathe. I think we offered the most acceptable form of general comedy, something to amuse most kinds of people without upsetting or insulting them.

You are always going to offend somebody. Slipping on a banana skin is such a classic joke that we did it, a joke on the joke itself, really *did* slip on one. In came a viewer's letter saying they'd slipped on an apple core outside their front gate and been paralysed for two years.

The sad part is that whatever you do, somebody will be hurt. I've had letters from stammerers, provoked by *Open All Hours*. When I opened one beginning, "We are a family of stutterers . . ." my heart sank but it went on to thank me for letting them fall about over their impediment, send each other up, and make light of things.

That does not excuse nor justify causing deliberate offence. Pushing back the frontiers of comedy? I'm all against it. Alternative comedy, so-called (in fairness, a lot of performers in that area hate the label), strikes me as an alternative *to* comedy; the material is done because they have no alternative! Swearing in comedy is the substitute for a funny line. Drop your trousers and you'll get a laugh, no doubt about it. Blaspheme and you'll get a laugh.

Television companies are so lax in what they allow that it amounts to anti-social behaviour. And the idea of the 'watershed' being nine p.m. is crazy. When did you last meet a child aged over eight, who goes to bed at that time? And eight to fourteen is the stage one should worry about, as a parent: that's when opinions are formed and standards absorbed.

Alternative comedy, 'uncompromising' drama and the like should go out at eleven at night. If those in the market for such material fall asleep before it starts, then hard luck – they must have enjoyed themselves in other ways!

Years ago our family was watching a BBC 2 play, a charming piece, and then suddenly two schoolboys started talking about disgusting, completely taboo subjects. I was so annoyed that I wrote to Aubrey Singer, who was running the channel, asking why in hell he didn't keep a little symbol on the screen so that people could avoid a certain kind of television. Everyone knows the embarrassment it causes – just as keen, probably more so, for children in a family group, as for their parents.

Aubrey's defence was that a warning was given before transmission. That's no good, because viewers, perhaps the majority, often switch on or switch over four minutes *after* the start. (That's why you never do your best jokes in the first four minutes, if you have any sense.) I was told the warning symbol suggestion was impractical; now they do do it.

"If you don't like it, switch off," is another glib answer. Too late, too late. You can't reach the set quickly enough. As for writers' and directors' tired old excuse about showing the way life is – people relieve themselves of waste matter every day of the year but we don't need to be shown it on television. "Reflecting real life" can be the easy way of doing without a story.

Rik Mayall and Adrian Edmundsen are charming men and can be charming actors. We had a long talk and I said that if they'd let me take four words out of their script they would get two million more viewers. Yes, they agreed, they were aware of that, but they felt a need to be hard, uncompromising. I wish they didn't . . .

All of which being said, I must admit that *The Two Ronnies* has been accused, by Mrs Mary Whitehouse no less, of "encouraging violence". That surprised you? We were taken aback, too!

What alarmed Mrs Whitehouse's monitors was Ronnie C. getting stuck in a revolving door during 'By The Sea'. Rikki Howard went wiggling past in a bikini, I trundled round in the door to get another look at her, and Ronnie shot out like a cork. The other incident involved lovely Madge Hindle, as companion to rather a grand lady played by Barbara New, getting a sharp prod from the *grande dame*'s parasol, for lingering over the postcard rack on the pier.

We'd assumed it was knockabout comedy. You decide. But if it was violence, then Laurel and Hardy, two of the greatest visual comedians in history, would be banned . . . and what about Charlie Chaplin? He kicked people all the time!

Final thought on the subject of television standards, to answer an obvious charge – no, I haven't become less permissive with age. I have become more permissive, like everyone else in Britain. There has been no choice, when you think about it.

21

UP IN SMOKE

THE bathwater was tepid because I had been sitting in it for an hour and a half now, singing all my favourite songs, then just any song coming to mind. Everyone sings in the bath, some time or other. But this bathroom was in the Queen Elizabeth Hospital at Birmingham. I was singing my heart out, scared that I might never be able to sing again.

Only a few days before I'd been singing 'Auld Lang Syne', seeing out 1971, a splendid year which had seen the first season of *The Two Ronnies*. That was off the air for the moment, freeing me for other things.

Jimmy Gilbert, a familiar colleague by then, had teamed up with Julian More, who'd helped write *Irma La Douce*, for a new musical. It was based on Falstaff, but a free adaptation set just after the turn of the century. Falstaff to Ragtime, and it was great. He comes back from a foreign war and moves in with his mistress, who runs a hotel, gets a drubbing while in disguise and so forth . . . *The Merry Wives of Windsor* but in another era.

When they asked me to be *Good Time Johnny* and said that Joan Sims, my chum from radio, would play Mistress Ford, I jumped at the project. We'd open at Birmingham Rep and, all being well, bring *Good Time Johnny* in to the West End. We all worked extremely hard, for this was an elaborate musical, production numbers, chorus girls, the lot. Joan and I had to learn several intricate dance routines. A month – January of 1972 – was set aside for rehearsals and after three weeks my voice started going.

At first it was no more than an irritation. *Good Time Johnny* had marvellous songs, I'd been using my voice a lot and assumed that after a while away from the stage, I was *mis*using it on all that singing. A fellow actor, lovely man, said his brother was a doctor who'd see me the following day, even though it was a Sunday, to prescribe a throat spray, lozenges or whatever. It never occurred to us that it was more serious than temporary hoarseness.

But I'd taken up acting and smoking on the same evening, all those years before at Oxford. Somebody offered me a cigarette, it was an adult rite of passage in those days, and pleased and flattered, I had lit up. A moderate smoker, twenty a day for a long time. For the last few years, though, it had become less moderate; life was busier, smoking helped concentration, so I was up to sixty a day.

The actor's brother examined me and said he would like a friend to take a look at my throat the following morning. The penny hadn't dropped yet, not really, but the friend was a specialist and he had been peering down my throat for a little time when he called, "Sister, come and take a look at this."

"Interesting," she said, neutrally.

I went cold. "I'm afraid you have a growth there which might be pre-cancerous," the specialist told me. He knew who I was, and after saying it wasn't too bad at the moment, asked when the Birmingham show would finish.

"Very well, in six weeks' time I'll trim a little piece off your vocal cords and have it tested," he explained. "Just to be on the safe side, though, come and see me next week."

It was disturbing news. There's no logic in this, but the idea of a heart attack, something which would fell you and that was the end of it, would have been easier to come to terms with. Cancer is such a spectre, it terrified me.

And from then on, rather like those nightmares which are all the more disturbing because they start calmly and turn ugly with frightening speed, the momentum increased. Somebody else got ready to play my part, I saw the specialist again and he decided, "We can't wait six weeks. You've got to come in tonight."

At the hospital he confirmed that I was a smoker and asked me to stop.

"When?" I asked. He checked his watch.

"Well, by midnight – I'm operating on you in the morning."

I got to my room at about seven in the evening and a nurse advised me to have a bath and go to bed, get some natural sleep before they started sedating me ready for surgery next day. Left on my own, I went into the bathroom, lay in the warm water . . . and started singing. It was a strange feeling. You always feel that it's going to be okay, at least part of your mind does. Still I sang everything I knew, in case it was the last chance.

When I came round the following afternoon, the specialist said the operation had been a success, so far as removal of the growth went, but the tissue still had to be tested to determine whether further treatment was needed. Very kindly, he promised to come back that night with the verdict.

"We got it in time," he told me, some hours later.

I wasn't allowed to speak for three weeks and had to write everything on a pad. "You can whistle but, for God's sake, don't whisper," he ordered me, which is worth remembering – apparently whispering is harmful if you're losing your voice.

There were worries still; a microscopic slice had been taken off my vocal cords and the surgeon warned that it could affect my voice, permanently. In the event, it did – I was able to sing slightly better afterwards.

152

There'd been warning signs. For months when my agent Peter Eade rang me, he'd ask if I had a cold. The phone was picking up that slight, progressive roughening of tone, but I hadn't taken it in. That was a long, lonely three weeks – Joy had to stay in London with the children, mainly – until getting the final confirmation that my voice was all right again, for speaking and singing.

One of the first things the surgeon asked, after the operation, was, "Have you still got your cigarettes?"

"Bedside cabinet," I scrawled on my pad. My lighter was in there, and rather a nice leather cigarette case, a gift from Joy, which I valued. He opened the drawer and pitched them out of the open window! We were several floors up, so somebody may have got a clout on the ear.

For a year afterwards I was in a desperate state. I couldn't write anything unless I smoked. But I dared not light a cigarette. Today it's different, I simply don't smoke and being around smokers does not bother me, they are welcome to go ahead. At the time, I used one of those dummy cigarettes, a little plastic tube containing menthol. That helped a lot – a dummy for a grown-up.

It was a struggle, though there was a comic side. "Drink a bottle of wine a night," said the specialist, when I told him what an ordeal it was, doing without cigarettes. I didn't drink wine at the time, but found that it was soothing, when I yearned to smoke.

About three years ago it came to me as I was opening a bottle – that specialist was an ear, nose and throat expert. "Drink wine," he said . . . he didn't care what happened to me below the neck!

22

NORMAN STANLEY FLETCHER

ANSWERING himself, Richard said, "There's nothing, absolutely nothing, when you die. It all goes black . . . finish."

I'll never be able to convey the poignancy of that conversation with Richard Beckinsale, Lennie Godber of *Porridge*. It took place about six weeks before his totally unexpected death from a heart attack in 1979. Richard was only thirty, and had just been declared fully fit after an exhaustive check-up connected with insurance on a film.

We were in a caravan, waiting for rain to stop so that we could do an outdoor location shot for *Porridge*, the cinema version. For no particular reason our talk turned to life after death, we'd discuss anything. I don't believe in God as a big, bearded chap somewhere up in the sky. Nor can I conceive of nothing for ever and ever. The dead may stop thinking for a million years . . . but what happens after that?

"You can't grasp eternity," said Richard. "Believe it, there's nothing."

He was a dear, sweet, funny fellow and his untimely death was the most awful shame. His wife Judy was in hospital at the time for treatment aimed at letting them start a family, and the news had to be broken to her there.

I can see him now, another evening when we'd both

had a few drinks. "You've got to stop this rubbish," he said, not knocking *Porridge* but meaning comedy in general. "When are you going to act? You're a great actor, I want to be there when you take on the important, tragic roles."

Normally we didn't talk about Acting with a capital A. He was like me; dare I say it – since for some people it's a derogatory term, though not to my mind – a jobbing actor. We were both natural actors, whatever that means. We liked to get on with it. But Richard was full of praise for me and I thought highly of his work.

"You'll be there," I soothed. Richard could be very insistent in his cups, wagging the finger, laying the law down. "You'll be there," I said. Heart-breaking, both of us so sure that a young man had all that time ahead of him.

Porridge was the best thing I ever did. I loved old Arkwright but Norman Stanley Fletcher was the role of roles. It's not being wise after the event to say we sensed that the programme would be special.

The genesis was a one-off by Dick Clement and Ian La Fresnais, *Prisoner and Escort. The Likely Lads* had been so good that we thought ourselves lucky to get them. They created Fletch for a comedy-showcase season I'd suggested titling *Six of One*, since another was planned for the following year and that could be *Half Dozen of the Other*. Since BBC comedy seasons last seven weeks they made it *Seven of One*. When I said they couldn't, it made nonsense of the sequel's title, the Beeb retorted, "Yes we can, we can call it what we like." And did!

Anyway, *Seven of One* launched three separate series, *Porridge, Open All Hours* and *The Magnificent Evans*, about a randy Welsh photographer. That never quite caught on, it was a bit too whimsical. Actually Dick and Ian wrote another one-off, *I'll Fly You For a Quid*, also with a Welsh setting, a clan of compulsive gamblers, and that would have made a fine series as well.

The great thing about Dick and Ian is their wonderful

stories: great characters and situations, just enough plot, and a very good ending. I've found out for myself as a writer that you must not bog yourself down with an elaborate plot; you can't cut the plot to fit the time, so the jokes get cut out. A crazy way of doing things but it often happens.

No question of that with *Porridge*, it was a success from the word go. The series was filmed at Ealing studios and because not only the famous comedies but several war epics were made there, it had an enormous tank built for water scenes in pictures like *Above Us The Waves*. ("*Above Us The Waves* . . . below us the Wrens," is the irreverent label somebody put on that naval genre.)

Drained, the tank became Slade Prison – empty, and treated by a brilliant set designer, there was room for the gallery (on ground level, actually) and the floor level, which in reality was the basement. Perfect perspective in the painting, plus very carefully aligned cameras, made everyone believe it must be a genuine prison location.

For the film, we did get a real prison. Luckily for the producers, there was a fire at Chelmsford jail – an electrical fault, nothing to do with the inmates – and the place was closed for renovation. Filming turned out to be tricky even though the prison was empty, as rebuilding went ahead, whether the film unit was present or no, so the noise was horrendous, with a constant crashing and banging.

We shot sequences whenever we could, at all hours, to use moments when the work paused. A little discreet bribery went on. The director's assistant, armed with a walkie-talkie, would stand beside some chap using a pneumatic drill, and when word was passed that the director was ready, the driller got a fiver and shut up for a few minutes!

Porridge started on 1 April 1973, good day for a joke, and though everyone thinks of it as having lasted longer, ran for only three seasons, between then and the begin-

156

ning of 1977. Even with two Christmas specials, that's only about twenty editions, but the series became a national pastime. Some prisons had to serve supper at a different time – so many prisoners missed the last meal of the day in order to watch the show, that food was being wasted.

The impact was brought home to me at a royal film première. Standing next to Roger Moore, I found myself being introduced to the Queen Mother. "Oh, they've let you out then," she said, and seeing my surprise at her knowing about the series, she added, "I watch it all the time, marvellous show."

I'm very patriotic (it seems unfair that one has to be a foreigner in order to be called an Anglophile!) and believe that the royal family does a splendid job for us. The Queen Mother's my favourite, though, for her terrific sense of humour and fun, and the fact that she's so in touch.

Some time later there was a royal gala at the Palladium and they rigged me out in flunkey's uniform to meet HRH in the foyer and hand her the special programme. *Open All Hours* had started, and I went, "Your puh-pah-programme, Your Majesty."

"Lovely, Mr Arkwright," she said, instantly. So staying in character, I went on, "That'll be two guineas, please."

Playing along, the Queen Mother looked at her pretty little evening bag and said, "I don't think I have any money on me." So I, or rather Arkwright, promised to send her the bill . . . VAT added!

That first jokey exchange at the première confirmed what *Porridge*'s audience ratings suggested, that it was something everyone watched. They didn't, of course, in some ITV regions it never got into the Top Ten; but it was unusually well liked. Everything worked out well – superb and consistent scripts, good chemistry between the regulars, on and off screen.

Richard Beckinsale wasn't my first choice for Lennie,

incidentally. I'd suggested Paul Henry, famous now as Benny of *Crossroads*. I'd been working with him on *Good Time Johnny*, the musical which finished for me when that cancer scare occurred. Godber was supposed to be a Brummie, Paul was Birmingham and he'd struck me as a clever young actor with a nicely cheeky face – Paul has put on a bit of pudding since then!

Fulton McKay had already been selected to play the crusty prison officer. I put Paul Henry's name forward but Sydney Lotterby, the director, explained that he was thinking of Richard Beckinsale, "A new lad, very funny, remember *The Lovers*?"

"Yes," I agreed, "but he's Nottingham and Lennie Godber is from Birmingham."

"Doesn't matter," said Syd, and of course it didn't. In early *Porridge*'s Richard tried to do a Birmingham accent but he gave up about three weeks in. For that matter, there was a big scar on my chin in *Prisoner and Escort*, the pilot episode, and though it was there in the first series, somehow it faded away and then disappeared for good, just like Richard's accent; and while Richard was working on his Birmingham and failing to get it right, dear old Fulton, Scottish as whisky, was fondly imagining that he was talking Cockney like me.

It's very difficult to produce anything worthwhile, let alone an enduring success, if two of the people involved hate each other's guts. My best trick has been ensuring, as soon as the choice was mine, that colleagues were likeable, *sympatico*. Ronnie C. and I always used to say, "Oh, don't have So-and-so, he's a terrible bore at rehearsals", or needlessly abrasive or whatever. People may be wonderful for the part but pains in the neck; there's always somebody else, equally good, and easier to get on with. It isn't self-indulgence or sentiment either. With television, there simply isn't time in the schedule to stop and explain everything, coax and reason people into things. When you are all on the same wavelength, more or less, then you deliver the goods.

Richard became a good friend. He was a very attractive man. I'm as heterosexual as the next man but there are men whose company is welcome, you're glad they are around, things seem better when they walk in, and it was that way with him. He was funny, charming, and an excellent natural actor.

Fulton, another close friend on the show, worked harder at it, worried more. You had to watch him, else three-quarters of a rehearsal would get taken up with his four-minute set piece! He agonised over his moves; once they were right, he was okay. It was funny, because Fulton was a highly skilled and experienced actor. Pitched onstage without notice, he'd have done fine, the famous moves would have been there.

"I can't play this scene, it makes no sense, it's unreal," he protested during one rehearsal.

Winking at Richard I said – but with a serious face, as if sharing wisdom – the first thing that came into my head. "Why don't you walk to the cell window, stand with your back to it, and deliver those lines?"

Fulton tried it, looked relieved, and said, "That's fine, I can do it now."

He knew *Porridge* was doing well, and that he was an important part of it, but Fulton didn't realise the scale of it. Then there was a charity performance, an all-star affair, presented circus-style in an enormous marquee. Several members of the royal family attended.

(The two Ronnies have never done a Royal Variety performance. Ronnie C. has appeared, and he's brilliant. I always felt that the honour and pleasure stopped with the invitation, then it was downhill all the way! After that, someone like me, who needs careful preparation and exact knowledge of what lies ahead, is on a hiding to nothing. Those special shows are prepared and put on so hurriedly that your act can be cut by half at the very last moment, and that would be a disaster for me; I have to know what I'll be doing.)

But this was different, both in setting and what was

159

proposed – just a brief appearance, a sort of elaborate sight gag. There was a huge audience, and in a pause between acts came news that Norman Stanley Fletcher had escaped from Slade Prison.

Cue for me to appear on a pushbike, pedalling furiously, hurtling round and round the outside of the ring. The crowd loved it, my feelings were what's tactfully known as ambiguous. Fletch doesn't wear glasses and I do. Without them, I had a dim impression of the outer edge of the ring bristling with struts and bars and ropes, accident after accident waiting to happen. But round and round I went, then came the sound of a police siren and the white van with the blue light roared in.

Out jumped Fulton McKay, in uniform. All he said, in that trademark bark, was *"Nobody move!"* The tent erupted, it was almost frightening; I'd been getting big laughs but this was a real explosion of laughter, affection, recognition, pleasure.

We leaped into the van together and off it went. The audience response came right through the metal walls. Close to tears, shaken and moved, Fulton whispered, "My God, they were . . . marvellous." Lovely moment, and I was so pleased for him. His eyes were opened at last to how popular he'd become.

Fulton and I shared another offbeat appearance which just went on and on, when he put the cuffs on me and it all went wrong. Being above feeble puns, I won't claim that it was an arresting situation . . .

During the run of *Porridge* the showbusiness fraternity, the Water Rats, made me their personality of the year. It meant a lot, that kind of recognition from one's peers, and I asked Fulton to share the award ceremony with me. After the show's first run the cast gave me golden handcuffs as a memento – not a jeweller's replica, these were the real thing, gold plated.

The idea was for me to turn up in character as Fletch, handcuffed to a disapproving Mr McKay. Fulton had another engagement that evening, possibly he was in a stage play, but it wouldn't take long, so he was game. We drew our uniforms from the BBC wardrobe department and set off for Grosvenor House.

Being actors, we wanted the timing to be right, so we hung around in the car until zero hour, in order to walk straight in and make it a genuine surprise. We snapped the handcuffs into place, and then it became flesh-and-blood cartoon sequence as Fulton jumped out of the car in his usual brisk manner and hurtled back inside as if on elastic. I'd managed to lock us together – with the centre armrest of the back seat between the cuffs!

Handcuffs are difficult to get out of at the best of times, which this was not, and the gold plating hadn't left any oil in them, so the key was stubborn. I fumbled, Fulton fumed, and after some five minutes we made our getaway, handcuffed together again, but without the car.

The award ceremony went a treat, Fulton hauling me in, and checking his watch and snapping, "Get *on* with it," at appropriate intervals during my acceptance speech. It wasn't all acting on his part, I was staying for dinner, but he had to be on his way.

Then we couldn't unlock the handcuffs. They would not come undone. We sat there like idiots, fiddling about, and it was forty minutes before Fulton got free and went haring off, leaving me still locked with handcuffs jingling. "Don't worry, I'm a member of the Magic Circle," said a Water Rat. "Have you out in a jiffy. You just have to know where to tap them."

He knew, arguably, but nobody had told the handcuffs. He tapped away and it was a toss-up which of us was more embarrassed. "This has never happened before," he kept muttering. I knew the feeling.

They unlocked in the end, and I have never turned the key in them again! A daft, hilarious night.

We all got on well together in *Porridge*, it was a hit, but after two seasons I was ready for a change. Quit while you're ahead – I had always been wary of getting stuck in a character. "But everyone loves it," said Bill Cotton.

"Let me try something else, all the same," I proposed. And that turned out to be *Open All Hours*. For a while people said, "Very nice, but we like *Porridge*." Then came yet another series and they missed *Open All Hours* . . .

All the same, Fletch may stay in certain memories long after his admirers have trouble placing Ronnie Barker. (*"Wasn't he on television . . . ?"*)

An actor can only bring so much to a part in the way of personal approach and attributes. There's a lot of me in Norman Stanley Fletcher but the character was created by Dick Clement and Ian La Fresnais. Be sceptical about talk of actors 'creating' characters. If the man's an executioner or an air-gunner, that's because it says so in the script. It used to irritate me when actors – actresses, more often – announced that they intended to play a part 'against the character' and make a dustman sound like a Guards officer. It's all in the script really, or most of it.

However, Fletch was based on my father, partly. He was a cheeky chappie, too, and could have been a leader. He had lots of repartee and backchat, and the same behaviour towards authority – outward agreement that was deceptive, not subservient at all. Certainly when watching old *Porridge* episodes on tape, I'm reminded of my father. We have the same nose too, but my sticking-out ears are my own, not inherited. I think it was the midwife, she must have used them for pulling me out backwards!

I could have carried on with *Porridge* after doing a season or two in a contrasting role. The BBC wanted us to, but after Richard Beckinsale's death I couldn't face it.

His passing, so suddenly and so young, was a terrible jolt. We'd been with him only the night before. Ronnie C. and I, and our families, were off to Australia for a year. If anything *The Two Ronnies* was even more successful in Australia, and the impresario Harold Fielding was taking our Palladium show to Sydney and Melbourne. There was a farewell party at Langan's Brasserie. All our friends came along, including Richard, but he left early because he had to attend another function. My last memory of him is sitting with Joy, teasing her, pretending to whisper sweet nothings. Then it was, "Cheerio, see you in a year's time – don't stay over there for ever," and he was gone, happy and full of life as ever.

When Syd Lotterby broke the news to us on the phone next day, Joy and I just put our arms round each other and cried. Syd had been in tears. Any death is tragic, but with Richard . . . He'd gone home that night, gone to bed, and just never woke up.

23

COME ON FUNNY

WHEN I was with the Oxford Playhouse company we'd go to the other theatre, the New, most Wednesday afternoons for the matinee.

One saw many pre-London runs there, and among them was *Blue For a Boy* with Fred Emney, marvellous Richard Hearne who made his name on television as accident-prone Mr Pastry, and Eve Lister. Often a bit of larking and corpsing went on at Wednesday matinees because they'd know people from the other company were in the audience. Fred would do the most outrageous things occasionally, anyway. That afternoon, in a scene where he sat on a park bench being serenaded by Eve, he surpassed himself.

He always wore these very voluminous clothes, capes and enormous, baggy checked suits. Halfway through her song's opening verse, Fred rummaged around among all the layers and solemnly produced a newspaper-wrapped portion of fish and chips. Equally solemnly, he proceeded to eat them. Fair's fair, he did offer her a chip when she paused for breath, poor girl!

Fred had a television series for a while in which he played a variety agent. In one episode an act came into his office – rode in rather, a human pyramid of three people poised on two bikes. They cycled round his desk, the woman juggling as she balanced on the men's shoulders. Fred didn't look particularly surprised or even interested. They went out, and after a masterly-timed pause he thought aloud: "I wonder what *they* do." Brilliant.

I love making people laugh and (this is a matter of record, not trumpet-blowing) I've had ratings, awards, compliments from colleagues and much reaction from people who've been entertained, to show that I've been able to do it. Just as importantly from my viewpoint, I love laughing. So before resuming the story, I want to celebrate some of the performers who've delighted *me*.

Fred Emney, of course . . . I liked him so much that a little of him, not least the monocle, is evident in my Lord Rustless. His forte was reaction comedy, he didn't have to do that much, just be there. Spectator comedy if you like, they make the humour out of what *they* are seeing. Groucho Marx is in the same sort of bag; apart from that peerless delivery, Groucho didn't care whether he was in the scene or not, he was wonderful as a spectator.

If asked to name the funniest thing of all, I would opt for eccentric dancing. I've always been a sucker for it, and eccentric dancing means Max Wall. He is the only man who has ever rendered me helpless, I fell off a sofa laughing at him. And Max Wall had that terrific don't-care attitude with an audience. Don't misunderstand, it wasn't arrogance nor contempt, not at all, but he was amusing himself as well as them. He could be eavesdropping on himself, in wry amazement, rather than in contact with people out there – in a world of his own. I've never forgotten one of his radio shows. "I like that joke," said Max, in his uniquely meditative way, "I like that joke, I'll tell it again." Which he did.

Nobody will ever approach the technical skill, and the charm of my two favourites, Laurel and Hardy. Oliver Hardy is charm itself when he's setting out to woo a lady – this big, fat man flitting about so lightly. Behaving in such a pansy way, not gay but a cissy, so fastidious when he flicks a drop of rain off his hat, a bit of fluff off his sleeve . . .

In their own field, Laurel and Hardy beat Shakespeare in terms of invention and output. They made thirty-two films, admittedly shorts, in *three years*. My younger son Adam and I are great Stan and Ollie fans, we've seen pretty well everything they made. That is how I realised the incredible output, film after film dated between 1931 and 1933. Writing, preparation, performing, Stan Laurel editing as well. How did they do it?

I admire Charlie Chaplin, one must, he's very clever. But Buster Keaton was cleverest of all; wonderful stunts, many of them dangerous. He doesn't make me laugh just by being there, though, it's the cleverness.

A great comic 'walks on funny'. His mere arrival is amusing. Tommy Cooper walked on, sighed, and you had to laugh. Same thing with Max Wall. Fred Emney had it. Most comedians aren't funny until they get started. Very few are funny as soon as they walk on. I'm certainly not and neither is Ronnie Corbett. Frankie Howerd, very funny performer, quirky, different, wonderful face, isn't in that category.

Morecambe and Wise, now they were. Eric Morecambe, in my submission, was the king of British comedy. Don't ask me what he had, because it was unmistakable yet indefinable. He simply walked on funny. I got to know him a little, we were friends and exchanged letters in the later years before his death. Eric paid me a compliment in one of his novels, saying that a fictional actress had "more awards than Glenda Jackson and Ronnie Barker put together"!

Eric devised jokes, cracked them, as easily and naturally as some of us breathe. He was great on the light-hearted put-down, the mock insult. It was all in fun, he was the kindest of men and only did it with friends. He came to dinner with us at Pinner one evening. Obviously we were proud of the house and Joy had knocked herself out to make everything look good; it was an occasion for us.

Eric breezed in with, "How are ya, how are ya?" Assessing the situation, his expression turned impish and in a stage aside to his driver, he said, "Come back for me in an hour."

Nobody else was in his class. You're allowed personal tastes but a line must be drawn somewhere, and you cannot say that you didn't like Morecambe and Wise!

My own concentration on comedy wasn't planned. It happened, and then other doors began closing for me. The public started associating me with certain kinds of programmes; they might be disappointed if I tried leading them along different paths and a perfectly good play or drama series could founder because of that. Personal considerations aside, that wouldn't be fair on everyone else involved.

My first and last classic on television was *A Midsummer Night's Dream*, for BBC 1 in 1971. I had reservations about it, but if there was any part I could play, then it was Bottom the Weaver. It has been played by so many comics. George Robey did it, among others.

It was well received as they say but I wasn't pleased with my performance, it wasn't strong enough. The play was done as an outside broadcast in the grounds of a stately home. Showing the difference between inside and outside viewpoints, Peter Black – doyen of TV critics then – felt it was enhanced out of doors, while I thought the method slowed everything down.

I wasn't very good as Bottom because I find Shakespeare's clowns almost impossible to play. This could be why countless perfectly bright people find them almost impossible to follow! You can only get laughs with Shakespeare's comics by doing things that aren't in the play – physical business and gimmicks, in other words.

And from the little experience I've had, I don't find classical drama enjoyable. I never had the vocal range or power to play characters like Falstaff, in my estimation. That hasn't stopped me getting a number of flattering invitations to try. Some years ago I was asked to play Falstaff in a straight drama series, *Lord of Misrule*. To my mind it was too late – I could have done it, perhaps, but for the reasons I've given, I felt that door had closed. Having been forced out of one Falstaff venture, at Birmingham, and turned down another, obviously I'm not meant for that part!

Jonathan Miller was insistent that I should be in one of his cycle of Shakespearian plays. Possibly he thought again, after I'd shared my heretical theories about Shakespeare. Laying out my argument that the comedy works only if modern business is imported, I suggested, "The alternative is to alter the script."

Dr Miller was startled. "You can't do that."

"Why can't you? Why don't you cut every Shakespeare play to two hours? He wrote an awful lot of rubbish, it means nothing to people today."

I wasn't winding him up, it's an honest opinion. Shakespeare *could* be cut, and a lot of scenes made more intelligible, less boring, and maybe, even funnier. I think that if Shakespeare was here today, he would be agreeable – he was a professional actor and dramatist, he would understand the problem. "Have a go," he'd say, "I was never happy with that bit myself, I was in a bit of a rush there."

Peter Hall kept urging me to join one of his National Theatre productions. "We are both older, wiser and happily fatter men than when we last worked together," he wrote to me fairly recently. "I am therefore making one last try to get you to the National – to play Falstaff in the two parts of *Henry IV*. You really should have a go, you know."

Perhaps I should have done. It wasn't timidity that kept me back. But there were sound reasons to doubt whether an audience would accept me. The doubt concerned whether I was right for such work any more. I hope I'm not pompous, how can I be, fooling around the way I have? But I wasn't embarrassed by anything I did, and was determined neither to have cause for embarrassment, nor to embarrass anyone else.

The offers kept coming along, however. To my surprise, I was offered the lead in a prestige drama series. It would have changed my image enormously, and the actor who did get the part made his name with it. Bill Cotton reminded me of my three-year contract with BBC Light Entertainment, so it didn't happen.

This isn't about the things I haven't done – for any of us, that would fill a shelf of books! But before *Porridge* emerged, Jimmy Gilbert was looking at series ideas for me and was very taken with a particular script. On reading it I understood why; there was a lot of great stuff in it.

"Terrific script," I told him a day or two later, "but it's all physical comedy, slapstick disasters, furniture collapsing, a loo disintegrating and so forth."

"Surely you could do it," said Jimmy.

"Yes, but somebody else could do it better. I'm a lines man, basically, and these are sight gags." Thank goodness I argued Jimmy Gilbert out of it, because *Some Mothers Do Have 'Em* became Michael Crawford's first television series.

Later I saw him on stage in *Barnum*, that extraordinary circus musical, and was so moved that I had to go round afterwards and tell Michael that his was the best performance I'd ever seen. All that energy and skill in so many different forms of performance, it was a phenomenal achievement. Other actors did it afterwards but Michael Crawford *was* that play when I saw it, he led the way and, for my money, was matchless.

Recently I went to *Phantom of the Opera* and congratulated him again. "Fantastic show – even if you weren't in it, it would be wonderful." Michael looked a bit nonplussed until I explained that he'd been tremendous in both productions but *Phantom* was so good that I could imagine somebody else doing it, whereas *Barnum* had needed him!

Whether my image made it inevitable or I just imagined that and turned the keys myself, the doors leading away from comedy were closed. I don't regret it in the least. There's something special about comedy, an extra spark. It's congenial for me, because I've experienced 'legitimate drama' as well as light entertainment, and light entertainment isn't as heavy going somehow. Performers involved in it tend not to get into discussion about capital-A subjects, Art or Acting. Nobody in the business believes that comedy is easier, the people doing it are just as intent on achieving peak performances, but by and large they get on with it . . . and have a bit more fun in the process.

Straight drama makes heavier weather of things, I suspect, because of directors' influence. The director in drama is much more important. Whether he needs to be as important is quite another matter. As an instinctive actor, I think there is a danger of over-direction in drama. Very naturally; the director feels it incumbent on himself to add something to a play, bring some personal element, instead of being content to steer his actors in the right direction. Direct them, literally. Sometimes he directs them along the road intended by the writer. The road's rarely hidden, by the way. It is there in the words. Often, however, a cast can be directed right off the map and off the face of the earth!

24

WINE AFTER WORK

PARTING from Norman Stanley Fletcher, at intervals from 1976 onwards I took to working for several weeks at a time in Helen's Beautique.

You must know the place. It's at Balby, Doncaster, Lister Avenue to be precise. Except that you may think of it as a certain corner shop kept *Open All Hours*. The BBC used to hire Mrs Helen Ibbotson's shop for a month or so. She went off on her hols and the Beautique turned into cunning old Arkwright's abandon-cash-all-ye-who-enter-here realm.

Open All Hours was great fun to do, and well liked. Audiences of nineteen million and more put it top of the national ratings. A survey established that Arkwright was considered Britain's funniest man. It should be pointed out that the research was commissioned by Bryant & May, seeking hints as to the best type of jokes for their matchboxes!

Despite his stinginess and the terrible way he treated poor Granville, Arkwright inspired a lot of affection. Possibly because *I* liked the old devil. And his money-making schemes were so small scale and eccentric, the whole neighbourhood shop thing so nostalgic, that you couldn't really disapprove of him.

My aim was to get away from Fletch, make people forget him while Arkwright was there. Arkwright's twenty years older, of course, but if you saw him and

Fletcher together in a pub, it should be plain that they're different men. In an odd way Arkwright is less real, though he's very solid, because there's his fantasy vein, the whimsy . . .

Again, he was created in the scripts by Roy Clarke, writer of *Last of the Summer Wine* and so much·else. His stinginess was there from the start, that terrible appetite for money, often in ludicrously modest amounts.

The stammer was laid on from outside. Roy asked me what I wanted to do with this character to whom he'd just introduced me. Looking for ways to make him different from anyone I'd played before, I thought of the stammer learned from Glenn Melvyn, some quarter-century before.

Roy was slightly taken aback, one could see him thinking, "*Stutter? I wonder why?*" but he told me to go ahead and try it. It was never in the same place twice, that stutter, but it worked. And it was a marvellous comic device as a help with timing – you could hold back on a word for exactly as long as was needed.

A lot of Arkwright was postcard humour, though not the explicit postcards of today. He was innocently sly, mildly ribald – ribaldry for family viewing. Nurse Gladys would be folded over, putting something into the back of her car, and he'd mutter, "Look at that, you don't get a buh-bah . . . boot like that on a modern car."

David Jason, Lynda Baron and I had some great times on that series. And filming part of it in Yorkshire – shop sequences there, the rest in the studio – made it even nicer because since my spell at Bramhall I've always been fond of northern people. They're genuinely friendly, witty, and down to earth. Somehow (this will get me into trouble) there don't seem to be as many strange people up north, there are more down to earth, common-sensical folk about.

We'd be there for only three weeks, doing the filmed sequences for two episodes each week. So work went on until midnight sometimes, with shouting, the noise of

172

equipment, and arc lights glaring. But nobody objected, though one chap did ask how long this would be going on for because he had to get up early for work!

The BBC generally found an empty house for sale and that would have the canteen on the ground floor, David and myself sharing one bedroom as dressing room and Lynda using the other. We'd put up posters and silly knick-knacks, make it homier, even though it was just for those three weeks.

Our trio's rapport showed in the spirit of *Open All Hours*. We were three mates. In the theatre one sees surprisingly little of colleagues, even during a long run. They're all arriving at different times, some needing longer to get ready, then the play's performed and everyone flits away again, wanting to get home.

But on location you all get together at the end of the day, have dinner, crack a bottle or two, relax and laugh. David Jason became a good friend. What a funny man. He and I have always had such rapport; ever since we first met at London Weekend TV in a half-hour comedy called *The Odd Job*. He subsequently played the hundred-year-old gardener, Dithers, in my series *His Lordship Entertains*, a show which I have always called 'Fawlty Towers Mark I', because it was all about an eccentric hotel run by my Lord Rustless character. Then he was in a few episodes of *Porridge*, and finally the long-suffering Granville in *Open All Hours*. What a wonderful sense of timing he has, with that marvellous rubber face. What a reliable and professional man to work with. I was so thrilled when he won the British Academy Award for best actor earlier this year

Lynda Baron completed the trio. She is marvellous company. She's bigger than Nurse Gladys – not physically, a lot of Nurse Gladys's padding got hung up on a peg in her dressing room, though the splendid bosom is genuine – but Lynda is a bit larger than life, full of energy, a showbusiness person. She's a marvellous dancer, incidentally, and used to be lead girl at the Talk of the Town when it was a cabaret showplace; recently she has been in the Sondheim musical, *Follies*. Very easy to work with, another one who wants to get on with it.

The three of us swopped anecdotes and experiences, teased each other, did a lot of talking and some damage to the *vin rouge*. Lynda had this stock line when debates started: "No one ever beats me in an argument, so don't try." David and I did try, though!

Another of my detours: I haven't had that many leading ladies in television comedy. There was no opportunity for one in *Porridge*, for obvious reasons. Fletch wasn't too happy about that . . .

I have known Jo Tewson the longest, she was in those early Frost programmes and the Palladium sketch for the BAFTA Awards which led to the BBC launching *The Two Ronnies*; Jo appeared in a lot of the Lord Rustless items and was co-star of my very last series, *Clarence*.

Her professionalism is admirable, Jo always knows every line, not to mention exactly what she is doing. Jo doesn't agree with me, but I think she lives to perform; a very theatrical lady, it means a lot to her. For years we've just been very close, affection on both sides, Jo is a joy to work with. She loves cricket, by the way. I enjoy watching it, despite preferring pontoon at school, but Jo's an afficionado, goes all over the place to attend matches, buys *Wisden* and collects all the books.

The Magnificent Evans – he was that flamboyant Welsh photographer, a sort of Orson Welles character – introduced me to Sharon Morgan. Evans was the sort of person who hasn't cropped up very often for me. Arkwright lusted after Nurse Gladys, in a wistful way, but Evans was successful with women and had this very attractive, live-in lover who was crazy about him, thought he was a genius, and let herself be exploited.

The in-joke there lay in Sharon being a fervent feminist. In fact she was a feminist, a nationalist and a Socialist, lots of *Ists*. Lovely to work with but goodness, we had

174

some terrific debates between shots, sitting in the car, passing the time with argument.

"Women are so much better than men," Sharon would say, and off we went . . . That was her doctrine, nothing about equal rights, just that men should be in their place – wherever that was. It was all good hearted, but couldn't she argue! That was half the fun of it, and she had a lovely name for the Department of Health and Social Security: the Department of Stealth and Total Obscurity.

25

PIGEON PAIR — PLUS ONE

WORK has never been the only thing with me. A lot of effort has gone into it, physical and mental, a big investment of time, concentration, thought. But at least half my life has been bound up with my family.

Just as I thought I loved Joy, only to learn that it didn't compare to the love that grew with our marriage, so I expected to love our children – having been one myself, I always liked them – but didn't know the half of it.

There's a saying that into each life some rain must fall . . . especially at the weekend! It is true, meteorologically speaking. So I ought to be worried about my life, it has been so lovely. But we did have a traumatic experience in the 'sixties with our elder son, Larry. This made me value my family even more, if that were possible, and put my work in a new perspective.

Larry was about five and a half when he got measles. It was unfortunate but seemed one of those expectable events, the doctor told us to keep him indoors, it was all quite low-key, a thing that happens. But Larry didn't get better, in fact he appeared to be getting worse, and weaker.

I have always felt it was my fault, that I should have been assertive. On the other hand, Larry was our first child, we lacked experience. I phoned the doctor, concerned, and he said the boy would be all right, just keep on with the medicine.

Then I got home from rehearsals one evening and Joy and I decided that Larry was really ill. The doctor came this time. "He's got pneumonia," was the verdict, "it can happen after measles." An ambulance was called, Larry was rushed to a local hospital and went straight into an oxygen tent.

It was harrowing. I stayed all night and they were pumping oxygen in and giving him penicillin injections. That made Larry scream, it was a big injection, a thick needle, and I'll never forget him screaming. Nor the awful, helpless feeling of watching this poor little soul who didn't know what was the matter with him or why he was being hurt.

Larry had contracted bronchial pneumonia. About three in the morning, another child was brought in, struggling for breath. He was much the same age as Larry and showed the same symptoms. After twenty minutes his parents emerged in tears, their son had died.

Sitting there, thinking about it, I glanced at Larry's oxygen supply . . . and the cylinder was empty. Frantic, I went to find a nurse. She was matter-of-fact, reassuring: "It's all right, ten minutes won't matter." Another oxygen cylinder was wheeled in on a trolley and brought up to the bed.

I could tell that something was wrong. *They couldn't open the valve.*

It was extra stiff and needed shifting, something to get some extra leverage. "There must be somebody . . . some way of getting it open," I pleaded. No, said the nurse, there was a porter but he was off duty for several hours.

Frantic, I got hold of the thing and somehow, with strength that was superhuman, made that valve move. I thought I wouldn't be able to; for a dreadful, timeless moment I thought it was not responding. I opened it, oxygen flowed. "Thank God for that," said the nurse, under her breath.

In the morning doctors examined Larry and said there

was a slight improvement. They told me to go home and get some sleep while Joy took up the vigil. I was driving back towards Pinner, the sun coming up. There's a house faced with Indian red tiles, and glowing in the sun their colour was so beautiful that I burst into tears. Had to pull over and stop, I couldn't see to drive.

That night had seemed to last a month but now the sun was out. It was a wonderful relief to have the feeling that Larry was going to be all right.

After a quick nap I went in to the BBC to the programme we'd been rehearsing the previous day – an age ago. It was *Crackerjack* with Leslie Crowther. As a relatively new parent it had been good to work with and for children. Suddenly it was an ordeal, having to go through with it while thinking of Larry's plight.

Two days later, sitting beside the oxygen tent in the knowledge that he was still very poorly, I could hardly bear to look at *Crackerjack* going out on a hospital TV set. The shallowness of comedy was brought home to me and I was filled with self-disgust.

It was unreasonable, illogical. Light entertainment gives countless folk a boost: the lonely, the elderly who can't get out much, handicapped ones who cannot get out at all, and people badly in need of diversion, cheering-up. Still it seemed wrong for this stupid comedy with me being silly, to go out while my son lay there so ill. I felt terrible. And it taught me to acknowledge what really mattered to me, the essential thing – my wife and family.

Everyone, every normal person, assumes that they'll be fond of their children. Then they arrive and you realise that you haven't imagined a tenth of the love that will be there. Larry's illness made us hypersensitive about all of them. One or other of us would slip into their bedrooms and time the breathing if there was the slightest cause for concern.

Larry's grown up to be a strapping big fellow, of course. Rather too big if anything, he takes after me! He is in advertising, works very hard, and is married to a beautiful girl called Julia.

First came Larry and then Charlotte, two years later. 'A pigeon pair', it's known as, a boy followed by a girl. And when Charlotte was about five, Joy said she wanted another child. We really differed over that, I thought she was mad. "You must be, we have two lovely kids and they're growing up, you're getting a bit more free time and independence, two is perfect," I reasoned.

"Don't care, I want another one," said Joy. Naturally she managed to persuade me! Put that way, it's a funny picture of Barker, feet dragging, being towed into the marital bower. There was no reluctance, not really, just my reservations over the added responsibilities of bringing up another child, and the added burden on Joy.

We were both delighted that she got her way, because Adam, our youngest – born in December 1967 – is a lovely lad. He's at York University reading English and Philosophy. He's interested in drama, not so much acting as directing. Though he's a good actor, we went to see him in a school play, *Hamlet*, and Larry failed to recognise Adam, who was rigged out in a beard I'd borrowed from the BBC!

I used to joke that being a first-generation actor was best . . . nothing to live up to. That didn't deter Charlotte. She started attending drama school during our year in Australia. She always wanted to be an actress. It won't be easy for her, the profession is even more crowded and competitive than when I began. But how could I warn her off? Yes, it can be frustrating, heartbreaking, but my knowledge of that is second-hand. Apart from that six-month lull between first and second jobs, and a bit of squalor and hardship in the mime company, my career progressed. Not always easily, a lot of hard work, but the same applies to any employment.

In any case Charlotte is like her mother, knows her own mind and gets on with things. There was never much question over her going on the stage. She faced higher barriers than I through the need to get an Equity card, of course. Eventually she got provisional union membership, allowing her to work in pantomime at Chipping Norton, where we live now. After three years of drama school, Charlotte did an audition for Julia McKenzie and was offered a part in *Stepping Out* on tour.

On opening in London it was a hit, but Charlotte needed a full Equity ticket for the West End – and had three or four months to get it before the play came in to town. To get full membership she had to do a minimum amount of professional appearances and somehow she scraped up the necessary weeks . . . Charlotte worked as an extra and was a cheerleader on *Top of the Pops* (one show's counted as half a week's provincial experience) and got into *Stepping Out* by the skin of her teeth.

We were thrilled to attend the opening night, she'd earned her chance. Charlotte played the nurse in the tap dancing class and, though I would say that, she was good. And in *The Children's Hour* at Derby, later, she was convincing enough to upset me. She was a disturbed, evil child and I found myself wondering where Joy and I had gone wrong, bringing up such a monster!

Another of Charlotte's jobs allowed me to hear one of the funniest remarks I have ever heard from a member of the audience. The production was a credit to all concerned, good performances, beautiful sets, well directed – but *The Reluctant Mistress* remained a very, very boring play. Naturally we kept our ears cocked in the bar at the interval to discover what people thought.

"This play hasn't been staged since 1780," remarked some knowledgeable person. That, or they'd read the programme notes. To which their companion responded, without hesitation, "*Why do they do it so often?*"

26

STOP AND SMELL THE ROSES

THAT last night, I wanted to break the ritual of so many years and so many shows by signing off with, "It's goodbye from him." I didn't say goodbye, it would only have started people wondering why the line had been altered, and wasn't worth it for the sake of satisfying a whimsical impulse.

It was December 1987, not long before Christmas, and though only a handful of people were aware of it, this was the end of *The Two Ronnies* for me.

The familiar payoff line, our finishing post for seventeen years, had been delivered and, off-air, we'd told the studio audience, "If you liked us, tell your friends . . . if not, remember, we're Little and Large."

The studio-cum-theatre started emptying. There was a little reception ahead, as usual, in Gerald Wiley's dressing room, but I lingered a little while. Already cameras were being stowed away and equipment being dismantled. For part of the team this was the real point of the evening, what they had been waiting for. (I've always found these special viewpoints wryly amusing; you can do a mediocre show but the makeup supervisor will say it was super, meaning it, because her wigs had looked splendid.)

Just another day for the suddenly busy people around me, they didn't know what it meant to me. Later, I stood in the car park, looked back at that giant concrete drum of the BBC Television Centre and said aloud, "It really is goodbye from me, then."

An emotional night, full of memories and nostalgia. Completing the pattern, my boyhood friend Ivor Humphris (the one who'd warned me not to get blasé) was there. Though he'd given up the stage and completed a career as teacher, he had kept his Equity card, so when he wrote to me on his retirement I arranged for him to appear in this final *Two Ronnies*. Even Ivor was unaware that having been in at the start, he was helping me bid farewell.

Why in the world did I retire at fifty-eight? The short and not wholly frivolous answer is, "Well, wouldn't you?"

Obviously there was a lot more to it than that. Mainly, I had no unfulfilled ambitions in any direction of show business. That may sound conceited but I hope that by now, you'll have gathered that I have a firm grasp on reality . . . and my own limitations as an actor.

And from the beginning I'd always tried to be different every time, never run a project into the ground, quit while I was ahead. After nearly forty years, that was virtually impossible. I could have carried on – piles of appreciative, very touching letters showed that people still wanted me – but in the end the material would be repetitive, probably less good.

Viewers don't say, "Ronnie Barker was good in a mediocre script," they say he wasn't up to much last week. I'd hate people to think of me as not as good as I was. That's always been important to me.

Above all, I wasn't enjoying it as much any more. When Peter Hall urged me to play Falstaff at the National Theatre, an opportunity which would have had me walking on air as a younger actor, my first thought was, "I'd have to fight all that traffic into London every morning, just to make rehearsals on time." And that told me something about myself.

The only reason for agreeing to embark on one last series, *Clarence*, was that as writer I could set it in Oxfordshire, ensuring that locations were on my doorstep. (The couple's cottage is based on one in the garden of our converted watermill home.)

Michael Grade understood. Once Ronnie Corbett had been told, I had to share my decision with Michael and my departmental bosses at the BBC, Jimmy Moir and Gareth Gwenlan. They didn't like losing a stalwart but I was determined that enough was enough. Michael wrote to me within a day or two: "I know what it is, you just want to stop and smell the roses." Lovely phrase.

There were reports, after I stopped doing *Open All Hours*, that my health was bad and I was cutting down on work out of fear of breaking down. That was nonsense. I've had a blood pressure problem for some fourteen years now but that's a condition, not an illness. It's controlled by pills which I must take daily.

Control, on the same amount of medication, gets harder with age, so my doctor ordered me to diet. Nothing novel in that, I have gone on diets, periodically, for as long as I have been an actor, trimming down before series. This time he told me to lose four stone, and I nearly fell over! However, I did take off three and a half, then gained a stone. Dieting is far easier when I'm not working – concentration matters, then, and one doesn't want hunger as a distraction. Retirement certainly won't harm my general health, but that wasn't a strong factor in giving up.

Is there life after entertainment, life after the BBC? Absolutely! Your job is not your life.

Among other things, I am retiring because I can afford to. Joy and I will draw our horns in a bit but should be able to live comfortably. Lord knows we worked hard enough. (I remember in the early days of the Frost shows, Ronnie Corbett appeared at a London nightclub until four in the morning, reported for David's rehearsals at ten the next morning, and grabbed a swift snooze before starting the entire routine all over again. "Ah yes, but it's another £35 a week!" he'd say.)

You don't become a multi-millionaire in this game, and there's no pension plan. What money there was left over went into bricks and mortar, speculation isn't for me. If I sold all the property I might just squeeze in as a millionaire – but where the hell would we live?

For thirty of the forty-odd years I was earning, there was eighty-three per cent income tax. Actors often get into difficulties over this, so I always put money aside to cover it. Then I got hauled before the tax man! Why, he demanded, had I not declared the interest on my savings this year?

"There is no interest," I explained. "All my money is now kept in my current account."

I had got sick of setting money aside for the Inland Revenue, receiving interest on it, then paying eighty-three per cent tax on *that* as well, plus fifteen per cent surcharge on top. A joke's a joke, but dash a pantomime . . . "I'd rather," I told the taxman, "get a smile from my bank manager of a morning, than be left with £40 out of £2,000 interest." He wasn't pleased, put my financial affairs through the wringer and learned what I'd known all along – that it was exactly as presented, no monkey business, just a point of principle.

Dealing with money isn't something I enjoy. Collecting things is another matter. It's in my blood. I still have one of the postcards sent to my mother from hospital before World War Two, and a King Edward VIII Coronation souvenir handkerchief given to me around the same time. The Duke of Windsor didn't make it but the hankie did!

The collector emerged, never to subside, when I was in short trousers. I'd play marbles for hours, to lay hands on a particularly fine specimen. There's a jar of them tucked away somewhere – not hoarded from that day to this, but bought years later, as an adult.

For me (I think) it's not acquisitiveness as such, else

184

I'd never let anything go. The attraction is in the nostalgia involved, solid tokens of the past. Just in case it *is* proof of an acquisitive streak, I plead guilty to trying to hook friends, so plenty of us can share the blame!

Years ago, knowing my tastes, Leslie Crowther gave me a Victorian arrangement of wax fruit under a glass dome, which he'd picked up on his travels for a quid or so. "You like all that kind of thing," said Leslie, adding, "You seem to get a lot of pleasure out of it, I might start collecting something myself."

Pot lids, I proposed, they weren't expensive – not then – every one represented a scrap of social history and had a story behind it. Now he has an outstanding collection.

If you happen to be a collector – and so many of us are – you'll know that the urge is hard to control. Some new interest just sidles up and buttonholes you, and you're done for. During the 'fifties, for instance, I was working at the Apollo Theatre and near the stage door was this book barrow. One passed it every day and there couldn't be any harm in glancing at the wares. I picked up a little book with period illustrations and found that it had been printed in 1815. My imagination was captured, something costing 2½p, known as sixpence in that era, had survived so long. It had to be rescued and given a good home!

That led to regular purchases, until the chap behind the barrow invited me to take a look at his storeroom, nearby. I went up and emerged with thirty-nine Victorian picturebooks for £2. I was a book collector and, in need, reluctantly, an occasional seller. Michael Gough bought a few, and I still wish I hadn't let them go!

At present I have fifty-three thousand picture postcards, some so valuable that they have to be kept in vaults. That started by accident, literally. I was appearing in *Lysistrata* at the Royal Court, sharing a dressing room with Peter Bull. He was a great corpser, by the way, and an even greater collector. His array of teddy bears was famous.

185

Now as ancients in *Lysistrata* we had to darken our bodies with liquid makeup called Armenian bole. It's based on earth, was once used as an ingredient of antiseptics, and had to be painted on, lavishly. Terrible job to get it off, too. One member of the cast never even tried, and started going green under the arms.

Sharing with Peter Bull meant that two large gentlemen, or too large gentlemen, had to busy themselves with the bole in a tiny dressing room. Hilarious but messy and, inevitably, I spattered the stuff on a postcard tucked into Peter's mirror.

"Don't worry," he boomed, when I apologised, but I did worry, and at the first opportunity, set off from the theatre along Kings Road. Sure enough, there was a shop with a box on a tray outside, and the box was crammed with postcards at one old penny each. All sorts of cards, views, comic ones . . . Jimmy Grout was with me and we riffled through, laughing at the Donald McGills and suchlike. The upshot was that I bought a hundred for a few shillings.

Collectors will understand the next bit. I had no intention of starting my own collection, that was Peter's hobby. I took them home to my flat and started sorting them out to give him next day and then it was, "Well, I'll give Peter *half* of these." *Irma La Douce*'s long run completed my downfall because at matinees I'd pop out to Cambridge Circus, a short stroll from the theatre, where there was another barrow run by a former ballet dancer who specialised in cards.

His cost as much as fourpence each in pre-decimal money and I'd scold him for being so pricey. But he provided the nucleus of my collection. Zena Dare, whom I worked with in *Double Image*, is on many of my cards, she and her sister Phyllis and Gladys Cooper were reigning beauties of their day, postcard queens.

I began with comic cards, funny and charming, and the bygone sweethearts, the Edwardian and 'twenties glamour girls, but now it has widened to view cards as well, often the only images of razed buildings or old streets.

Postcards, illustrated books, prints, *objets d'art*, some posters. It's not that big a collection, really, I refuse to brand myself a hopeless case. In Australia Larry and I enjoyed playing the American pintables and I did bring three of them home with us, but that doesn't count. He said!

When Joy and I had been married for a year, it didn't take much working out that we could start buying a house for half the weekly outlay on our flat: eight guineas rent against four guineas mortgage repayments. That would have been around 1958, and we found a little semi-detached at Alperton for £2,800. That got us on the ladder. And we'd drive around in our first little car, an Austin A40, often travelling out through Harrow to look around Pinner, which we liked. There was one house, an older place in Church Lane, Pinner, which we loved. "Wouldn't it be nice to live there," I'd say, and Joy would reply, "I think we will, one day." We always laughed, because the house was not simply out of our league but wildly beyond our hopes.

Eventually we did move to Pinner, settling there. We'd still looked at 'our house', it was only five minutes away now. About six months after agreeing that we'd stretched our resources, especially with a family to bring up, and couldn't possibly move again, the Church Lane house came on the market. It was nearly twenty years ago and the price was £23,000. That struck us as a fortune, really daunting. But we were shown round and were enchanted. We made an offer, the estate agent said somebody else had made a better one, and that seemed the end of the matter.

"Fine," I said, and we went home. It was a weekend, the sale would be clinched the following Monday. Sunday morning I was having a bath and thought: *"We're going to live there."* A quick conference with Joy led to us contacting the estate agent at home, and we agreed to pay the full asking price.

We were so pleased with it that there was never any question of moving until my retirement. New House it got called when the place was extended, but in fact it is quite old. Lord Nelson's illegitimate daughter Horatia lived there as an elderly lady. So, but not at the same time as Horatia, did another Barker – Sir Herbert, a celebrated bone-setter and no relation. George Black, a famous impresario with his brother Alfred, was another owner. Oh yes, and Elton John used to deliver the papers, when he was little Reg Dwight and lived in Pinner.

It had a lot of rooms and plenty of room but, on the other hand, over the years I collected plenty of postcards, books and illustrated magazines. One day I came home from an auction with something rather large and extensive in the antiques line and Joy, as wives will, said, "Either we get a bigger house or we'll have to start a shop."

"Good idea," I agreed. So we did both, opening The Emporium in Chipping Norton High Street and finding a house to retire to a few minutes' drive away.

27

GOODBYE FROM HIM

PEOPLE thought it rather eccentric when I didn't announce my retirement, but left a message about it on my answering machine.

I thought it perfectly sensible. Anyone ringing to offer me work would find out that I wasn't available. An official announcement struck me as a bit much – I wasn't important enough for that and neither was the event.

But then the letters started coming in, after the press caught on and ran stories. It's hard to explain, but despite being aware that I was highly paid and the shows were successful, I couldn't consider myself 'a star' . . . they were other people whom I admired. I'd still dash across the street for certain autographs!

Maybe my mind was closed to the fact of popularity. Take too much notice, allow it to bulk too large, and it can be harmful. At the best, you take yourself too seriously.

When Larry and Charlotte were small we could do things as a family, go to the zoo, have picnics and outings, without notice. By the time Adam came along, things were changing. We had this holiday house at Littlehampton and at weekends Joy could stay on the beach with the children but I had to be indoors – I'd watch for their return and put the kettle on.

It's fine for people to stare, come up and start talking, that's a product of success in one's work. "It comes with the territory," as the Americans say. So you accept it and, indeed, think yourself lucky. But it means that what you have set out to do, such as taking the kids out for a treat, changes nature and you're on duty and on display.

I remember an August Bank Holiday at Littlehampton, when it just wouldn't have been sensible to go outdoors. The place was packed. It was midnight, and I mean midnight. "I must get a breath of air, I'm going for a stroll on the beach," I told Joy.

And as I stepped out of the front door, a car braked hard, four youngsters tumbled out and cried, "Ooh, it's Ronnie Barker!"

Joy and I went to Paris, our first visit, and did the obvious, went to the Louvre to see the Mona Lisa. There was a big crowd in front of it, naturally, and we stood on the fringe. And then Joy nudged me *and nobody else was looking at the Mona Lisa*. They were a British tourist party, mainly, studying me studying the Mona Lisa!

There was a lot of that. Perhaps it's just as well that I keep remembering funny things, silly things, which prevent delusions of grandeur. Soon after coming to London I auditioned for a revue, unknown country for me.

You go into a theatre in the middle of the day, which is quite daunting. I never had much luck with auditions. Anyway, I tried them with a parody from a *Kismet* number. *'Take my hand . . . I've still got another one,'* making a grand gesture which sent my false hand sailing right out across the stalls.

"Thank you very much – do you want your hand back?" was the icy response.

And there was the night I nearly got myself arrested.

Prince Charles was being inducted into the Water Rats, Ronnie Corbett had been invited to make one of the keynote speeches, and Bill Cotton thought it would be a grand idea for the Other Ronnie to make a surprise appearance.

The ceremony was being held at the Grosvenor House

Hotel in Park Lane, I got hold of the authentic waiter's gear and slipped in once the event was under way. Nobody recognised me, here was just another waiter, and I started sidling along a side wall, getting nearer and nearer the top table . . .

That was when Prince Charles's security men pounced on me! If I'd spent the rest of my natural life in the Tower, the BBC would have been to blame . . . However, my wig and moustache disguise didn't take too much penetrating and they let me do some more sidling.

Ronnie C. started sparkling away with his address (I'm hopeless at that, unless on stage or in front of a camera I go to pieces, the grey mist comes down) and then this surly waiter, anxious to finish his shift, started grabbing plates and muttering, "Finished with this, 'ave yer?"

Prince Charles caught on at once but certain VIPs were outraged, taking it seriously. Sir Billy Butlin was glaring at me, willing the idiot waiter to vanish. Especially after I dusted his collar free of imaginary dandruff . . .

Afterwards, Prince Charles told me one of his favourite films was *Futtock's End*, a silent comedy of mine, which was gratifying. And when Ronnie C. and I were awarded OBEs in 1978, the Queen told me, "What you do brings laughter to an entire nation."

If true, I have been amply rewarded. And not only in obvious ways. Sir Alec Guinness's autobiography, *Blessings in Disguise*, was published a few years ago. Now there *is* an actor – and I was amazed, delighted, to turn a page and find: *"I'll tell you who my favourite performer is. Ronnie Barker. Surprised? You shouldn't be. He's really great."*

Surprised was not the word!

Another unexpected compliment was paid on television, though never screened. The producer sent me a taped snippet from Terry Wogan's show, cut for time reasons. Now I'm genuinely starstruck, bowled over by certain entertainers, and Gene Wilder comes high on that list. So it was a thrill to play the cassette at home and watch him saying, "I lived in England for a year while making a film here, and *The Two Ronnies* was my favourite show. I thought Ronnie Barker was maybe the funniest person I ever met in my life."

Lovely compliments, just like those viewers' letters, so full of affection, gratitude, goodwill that one had a sense of discovering friends, as distinct from being well known through television.

I'm glad that they enjoyed what I did. I wouldn't have dreamed of doing anything else. Nothing else could have given me so much fun, pleasure and fulfilment.